WHAT'S HIS NAME?!

DIDN'T YOU USED TO BE WHAT'S HIS NAME?

by Denny Miller
(aka What's his name)

Stay Healthy!
Denny Miller

I'd like to share the smiles in life
wrapped up in the coat of comedy
under the hat of humor
wearing the ring of laughter
with my feet firmly planted
on the mirth

D.M.

DIDN'T YOU USED TO BE WHAT'S HIS NAME?
by Denny Miller

Printing History
First Edition, September 2004

Manufactured in the United States of America.

ISBN 0-9753917-0-4

Published by

TO HEALTH WITH YOU PUBLISHERS, LLC
8550 W. Charleston Blvd., #102-374
Las Vegas, NV 89117

Designed by

Brian J. Bohnett
Mad Kings Publishing
1909 Chestnut Street
Holt, Michigan 48842

CONTENTS

FOUR WORD

PLEASE READ THIS BOOK!

PREFACE

TV commercials have been assuring us for many years that participation in team sports during our formative years prepares us for a good life. Denny Miller is living proof of the truth of this assertion. There's not a mean bone in his body, although "funny bones" abound in his six-foot four-inch frame. His book is a candid look backwards, through humorous anecdote and sober observation, at a life he has lived with good sportsmanship, ready humor, and a healthy appreciation for the many role models met along the way. At the top of the list is his father who served on the Advisory Committee on Physical Fitness for Presidents Eisenhower and Kennedy. His UCLA basketball coach, John Wooden, runs a close second. They both helped mold a receptive candidate into a model citizen. Denny's good nature and concern for others did the rest.

There have been many athletes-turn-actor whose life stories are worth exploring. If, like Denny, they apply the rules of their sport to the rules of the acting profession, the results are always interesting. The two worlds are not mutually exclusive. Denny's book is divided into easily digestible segments, each with a subject heading, and framed in a general chronological pattern. Readers will have a few guffaws as they follow his odyssey through life with anecdotes of his fellow actors like Peter Sellers, Katharine Hepburn, Jack Lord, Bette Davis, Chuck Conners, Lucille Ball, Sidney Poitier, and many others. He also explores the hazards of shooting on location, giving us a first-hand account of what actors endure to create realism on the screen. From "Tarzan" to "Gorton's Fisherman," Denny Miller has made lasting friends through good humor, good sportsmanship, and playing by the rules.

George T. McWhorter, Curator
Burroughs Memorial Collection;
Editor: Burroughs Bulletin

ACKNOWLEDGMENTS

I thank George T. McWhorter for editing this book. I know being editor of the Burroughs Bibliophiles and Curator of The Burroughs Memorial Collection at the University of Louisville takes thirty-eight Earth hours a day. I have suspected for a long time that George originates from one of ERBs' other worldly stories. His daily workload proves I have been right.

Thanks to Nancy Gordinier for her ideas and for typing copy after copy on the computer deleting my many mistakes. She has a degree from the University of Miami, where she was on a Journalism scholarship. She has the largest degree of my love. She is a caring, compassionate person with an enthusiasm for life, love and laughter.

I thank all the people at GORTON'S especially CEO Steve Warhover, Mark Lamothe, Judson Reis and Jodi Nedro-Counihan. They gave me a second chance to have the dignity that comes with the holding of a responsible job with their successful company. With that confidence builder I started to write.

Thanks to Bob Gorman for a final push, "GET ON WITH IT!" he said. Thank you to Gretchen Smith, for doing the final edits before going to print. And, thanks to Brian Bohnett, of Mad Kings Publishing, for designing this book.

And I thank me for having the sensibility to be aware of my debt to these people; and feeling strong enough about it to make a small repayment in writing.

I would also like to thank all those individuals who provided photographs for inclusion in this book. They are: Gorton's (pages 2 and 176); George T. McWhorter (pages 11, 98, 117, and 159); Coach John Wooden (pages 29, 31 and 33); David Fury (page 40); Rafer Johnson (pages 43 and 44); Michael Burns (page 58); Boris Vallejo and Julie Bell (pages 118 and 119); Fred Causey (page 133); Judy Yeager, (page 152); Dick Gautier (page 155); and David Moss (pages 166, 168 and 169). All other photos reproduced in this book are from the author's collection.

INTRODUCTION

These days my resident librarian goes on longer and longer lunch breaks. When this happens and it happens everyday, I'm "out to lunch" too.

So I needed a place to jot down some memories of names and faces that crack a smile on my cracked face.

This book turned out to be that place.

Five former Tarzans: James Pierce, Johnny Weissmuller,
Buster Crabbe, Jock Mahoney, and What's His Name (1975).

CHAPTER 1
WHAT'S HIS NAME?

Every time you turn on your TV, you invite an actor or a bunch of actors into your home; right into your living room, rec. room, kitchen, back porch, bedroom, even into your bathroom at some hotels. It happens all over the world. Granted they are in a box, they're flat, sometimes black and white... but there they are.

Day after day, night after night, for hours at a time they're there. This has been going on for many years. Some of these actors are practically members of your family. You spend more time in their presence than with your kids. In the U.S., the average time spent watching TV is somewhere between four and seven hours a day. Between soap operas, the news, unreal reality shows, sit-coms, sporting events, documentaries, detective series, home repair, cooking shows, interview programs, kids programs and movie reruns, who has time for much else?

It's no surprise that when you see these actors at the grocery store thumping a watermelon, or pumping gas next to you, or sitting behind you at a ball game, you recognize them. They've been in your home almost every day for years. In person, they may be shorter than you thought, or have no beard or are bald as a banister, or have lost their limp or gained one, or are not as snappy a dresser as they are on screen. But there they are; round not flat and in color, with moles and nose hairs and all the other imperfections that make-up hides.

There's your old friend that you've had lunch with, that you have listened to from another room while you ironed a shirt, that you've fallen asleep with... but what the hell is his name? He's played so many different characters. I liked him years ago on that Western and in that Gorton's Popcorn Fish TV commercial... What IS his name?

Here he comes—don't be shy—say hello—thank him for all the laughs, "AAAAAA—Pardon me... didn't you used to be what's his name?"

Denny

 # CHAPTER 2
CATCH 21

I got dishpan hands for my twenty-first birthday. That's what you end up with when you wash thirty-eight billion trays three times a day. I was on a troopship headed for Germany. We were on a two-year expedition in the year 1954. I started the trip on KP.

It was the worst of times and it was the worst of times. I had just spent sixteen weeks learning how to kill at Fort Ord, California. We called it Fort Consumption By The Sea. Most of us got the flu from the daily fog floating in from Monterey Bay.

We were "Ground Pounders," U.S. Infantry. We were going to occupy Germany. Germany was already occupied by Germans. But we were occupation forces so that's what we did for an occupation. Most of us were only going to be there for two years. Just long enough to acquire a taste for German beer and wiener schnitzel and ladies with hairy legs.

No one was shooting at each other so it was not a dangerous job. If we had been shipped west from Fort Ord, we'd have ended up in Korea. In the company I trained with, they (whoever they are) divided us at the space between the L's and the M's. Everyone whose named started with the letters A through L went to Korea. Miller to Zabroski went to Deutschland. If my name had been Brown, I wouldn't be writing this.

They called the Korea thing a police action. Those guys didn't even have the honor that goes with fighting in a war. It was a very sad thing and lots of them got dead being policemen in khaki. I hate war!

> ## "It was the worst of times and it was the worst of times..."

Today, almost fifty years later, Korea is still smoldering and Germany is still being occupied. A half a century of GI's stationed in Germany. Wonder how much that cost?

After eight days and twenty-two zillion more trays washed, we landed in Bremerhaven, jammed into a train and went straight to Bavaria to play war games. That's when thousands of soldiers run around in the snow shooting blanks at other GI's.

The second day there, a sergeant approached our squad while we were waiting to shoot more blanks and asked if any one of us knew anything about radios. I jumped up with a

G.I. in Germany.

solid, "YES!" So did five other guys. We all marched over to meet our Captain. He was looking for a new radioman. The Captain's radioman followed him around carrying a twenty-two pound metal radio box on his back. He had one there.

It was covered with knobs and switches and dials and had a three-foot aerial sticking out the top. I was the tallest volunteer there, so I got the job. That seems like a logical decision. Not so. Thank goodness we weren't asked to demonstrate how to use the thing. I didn't know how to turn it on. I found a manual and studied the contents that night.

"The woods were full of blackberries. War had to wait. After all it was just a game."

As the Cap's R-man I got to ride in the back of his jeep. You really save on shoe leather doing that. Out in the field, and that's where we were most of the time, I got to sleep in the jeep's little trailer. The camouflage nets were kept in there and made for a much softer bed than a hole in the ground; much drier also because the trailer had a lid in case of rain.

The war games came to an impressive finale. Well, they were supposed to end with a bang. Our infantry company, along with thirty other companies, was to take a large Bavarian hill. We had artillery support. Once that stopped, we were to charge up the hill, through the woods, roar into the clearing at the hill top, and take up positions (dig fox holes) and wait for the all clear signal.

Everything was going well. Our company was fanned out, rifles at the ready, advancing up the hill. We had a good view of the attack from the captain's jeep. They came to the last thicket of woods and were swallowed up in its darkness.

The Cap told the driver to drive on up the dirt road one hundred yards where the troops would charge out into the open and take the summit. At eleven hundred hours, it was time for the last push. No troops—not one. A minute passed and still nobody came out of the woods. Radio silence had been called for. No one was to use his radio. After two more minutes and no charging infantry the captain grabbed the radio from me and broke some rules. Remember, radio silence means you're not to use the radio; he did. You're not to use profanity; he did. You're not to use the names of his officers; he did. No answer, not even a squeak of static.

He threw down the phone and just as he jumped out of the jeep we saw movement. First one, then three, then a bunch of guys straggled out of the thicket. Their mouths were black.

The woods were full of blackberries. War had to wait. After all it was just a game.

The games were over and the company was back at base, a place called Kirch Goens. We lovingly called it "Sheep S--- Hill." It was fall, a beautiful day in Germany. Football season was in the air. I had had enough war games. It was time to play a game I liked. The day after I had filled out the application form to try out for the football team, my company headquarters

A tight end on a loose team.

got a phone call for me to report to the base gym and to the Major that ran Special Forces. He wanted me to coach the team.

I hadn't played football for four years. The last time was when I was a junior in high school. I might have stretched the truth on my application form. I might have mentioned playing for UCLA. I did play basketball there, an easy mistake. Anyway, I told the Major I'd rather play than coach.

The first day of practice I was in the locker room an hour early. I wanted to see how the thigh pads were supposed to go in their pockets. I didn't want to put shoulder pads on backwards. I would make a good spy. I got the whole uniform on right.

My company C.O. wasn't thrilled that I had opted to leave the radio job. He had been grooming me for an appointment to West Point. When you're the Captain's radioman, you're not on the duty roster, so I hadn't stood guard in the snow or done kitchen duty. The day after Cap found out I was planning to leave he put me on guard duty.

I shined my boots and sharpshooting medals and marched off to stand guard in the knee-deep snow. Thirty minutes later I strolled back to the company area. I had been chosen Colonel's orderly. That means I didn't have to stand guard and instead got a three-day pass. GOTCHA, Cap!

I played very hard so I wouldn't have to go back and face KP and guard duty. I knew my captain would be waiting. I caught so many touchdown passes I made honorable mention on the All-Army team. I really didn't enjoy washing trays.

After football season came basketball season. Our team was average but we got to travel around Europe playing other bases. After basketball season, I had reached the magnificent rank of Corporal and was placed in charge of the gym by the Special Forces Major. I never did go back to my company. I even sent a buddy back for my mail.

The army experience turned out well for me just because my name started with an "M." In this day of an epidemic of overweight men in the U.S., it might be a good idea that our country follow the example of Switzerland. When a Swiss man reaches a certain age, twenty-one I think, he is required to go in the army. All Swiss men go through the training. No one is excused, not even politicians' sons or cousins or nephews.

Just imagine what army training would do for our legions of couch potatoes. Five or six months of fitness programs would do wonders for our soft, out-of-shape, overweight men. After they completed training, they would return home feeling better than they ever had. They would be stronger, healthier and have much more pride. What a concept.

While stationed in Germany, we sometimes trained near German troops. We used to talk with each other over a knockwurst. One German soldier told me that during WWII the German soldiers used to sing a song that went like this, "Switzerland, Switzerland you little porky pine, we'll get you on the way back."

I hate war. I hate fighting of any kind. But I'd be more comfortable in my AARP years living in a country that had a few good men under fifty that were porky pines instead of two out of every four men being a marshmallow. Many of our able-bodied men are still occupying Germany.

Not that we were anxious to be discharged when we tumbled off the troop ship in New York. We wanted to be flown back to California. It took seven hours to fly at that time. The train took two and a half days. Taking a plane we'd be civilians two days sooner. We boarded a train.

> **"It took seven hours to fly at that time. The train took two and a half days. Taking a plane we'd be civilians two days sooner. We boarded a train."**

In Chicago we were transferred from the troop train to a civilian train. I was assigned to a private compartment with its own sink and john. Some one had made a big mistake putting a Corporal in his own room. Naturally, I complained... NOT!

Things like that come under the heading of: "last name begins with 'M'; being tall enough to carry a radio; eating blackberries with the troops; being the colonel's orderly; not putting a football uniform on backwards."

Call it dumb luck or call it "a catch 22" or call it "a snafu," call it what you like. I call it all three. I enjoyed my solitude all the way to San Francisco. I was a semi-civilian two days early. I even treated myself to a German beer with the last dollar I had in my pocket.

CHAPTER 3
LET ME SEE YOUR HAIR-LINE

Moving furniture is a pain in the back. But that was my summer job putting myself through college. UCLA tuition was a bargain compared to other universities and a good summer job, plus my athletic scholarship paid for my education way back in the fifties.

I had worked one summer for Carnation Ice Cream. My job was to go in the freezer, thirty-five degrees below zero, work for half an hour stacking five gallon containers of ice cream and then come out into ninety-plus degree heat and work half an hour. We worked in two-man teams, alternating in and out each hour. I worked there about two months. In that time, I had eight different partners. They all quit. One guy lasted half an hour. He said he had applied for a truck driver's job and there was no way the freezer looked like a truck.

Tough test.

I didn't quit. But I should have. I had chills and sweats for months after working there. I guess my body wasn't very tolerant of working in temperatures that varied 140 degrees sixteen times a day. DUH!

Moving furniture was a much better job. We were loading office furniture from a warehouse into our truck on a nice sunny day on Sunset Boulevard in Hollywood. I was pushing a desk chair on its casters to the truck when I heard, "Hey you!" I turned to see a guy leaning out of his car window. He had stopped by the curb.

"Me?" I said still holding onto the chair.

"Yeh, come here and let me see your hair-line," he yelled, so I could hear him above the traffic noise. I couldn't believe that I had heard what I just heard, but out of curiosity I gallunked over to the curb and pulled my hair back out of my face.

"There ya' are," I said and I turned back to the chair. By now I figured it was some kind of joke, and besides my boss was in a hurry to get the stuff loaded.

Over my shoulder I hear, "Here's my card. Give me a call." I turned around, took the card, and off he drove. I even remember the make of his car. It was a Karman Ghia.

The card read "Robert Raison. Talent Agent."

I put the chair in the truck and went back in the warehouse. "Where the hell have you been?" he asked.

"Well you're not going to believe this, but a guy just..."

"We don't have time to goof off. Put the rest of this stuff on the truck!" barked my boss, Mike.

I followed his command, having just been discharged from two years in the US Infantry in Germany. It was second nature. Someone barks an order, I do it.

I'm not making this up. Another chair, outside on the sidewalk, another guy. He gives me his card. Same occupation. I don't mention this second guy to Mike; he's pissed off already. Mike spent most of his time being pissed.

Well, we got all the desks and desk chairs and office lamps loaded and Mike drove to the offices. It turned out to be a theatrical agency... five or six offices... five or six agents. I ended up with three more business cards.

Nothing like this had ever happened to me. Never has since. I took it as a joke. I'd heard of Lana Turner being discovered in a drugstore on Sunset Boulevard. But I was going to be a basketball coach, high school or college. I broke into a sweat at the thought of giving a speech in speech class. Telling jokes to buddies was the extent of my show biz experience.

After work I went home and put the five cards in my sock drawer and forgot about them.

A few days later when I showed up for the day's work at Bekins Van and Storage, the dispatcher handed me a note with a phone number and a name to call, Robert Raison, the guy in the Karman Ghia. I threw it in the trash and Mike and I moved furniture.

The next day – same kind of note, same trash basket. The third day, Jim the dispatcher, gave me another note but added, "If you don't get this guy off my case, you're fired!!" That got my attention.

I called Mr. Raison. He talked me into coming to his office just to read a scene from a film called "The Cowboy and The Lady," an old Gary Cooper film. I said I would after he promised not to call Bekins again. I needed that job.

Life is what happens to you while you're on your way to do something else. Mr. Robert Raison, agent, got me two screen tests, a contract at Review Studios (soon to become Universal Studios) and a contract at MGM, and was my agent for fourteen years. I'm indebted to him for forty-five years of a life I had never dreamed of.

Back at UCLA that fall, I offered to loan my Bekins uniform to my fraternity brothers who were studying theater arts. I also suggested that maybe, just maybe, they ought to change their majors to physical education.

17

I used to be Denny Miller.

CHAPTER 4
A TEST?

Hollywood Screen Tests... The first one I took was what they call a "Personality Test." Or at least that's what they called them back in the fifties. The actor or actress stands or sits in front of the camera and follows the director's commands.

"Please introduce yourself." (I didn't say it was a tough test.) "Let us see your right profile, your 'OTHER' right profile. Now the left one."

"How old are you Denny?"

Me: "Twenty-four."

Director: "And are you an actor?"

Me: "No. I'm a student/athlete at UCLA. I'm on a basketball scholarship and studying for a degree in physical ed."

Director: "Have you ever thought about being an actor?"

Me: "No."

Tough test. For remembering my name, I got a seven-year contract at Review Studios (later known as Universal Studios). I told them I wanted to finish my senior year in school, so they said if I would come to the studio several times a week for free acting lessons, they would start my contract the day after my graduation.

Me: "Okay."

Personality tests show how the person photographs, how his voice records and lets them know if you freeze in front of a camera.

There is another kind of test. This one you actually do something. You do a scene for a specific role in a movie or the job of spokesman for a particular product. It's an audition on film. You act, or you hope that your acting fits the role they are trying to fill.

I've done both kinds of tests. I passed a couple and flunked several. The screen test for the role of Tarzan at MGM Studios was the acting kind. It was also one of the silliest screen tests ever made.

I don't know how many guys they tested. I was a contract player at MGM at the time, which meant that if I did get the role, I would be cheaper than the chimp and much cheaper than the elephant. I made $180.00 a week as a contract player.

A friend, Bill Smith, was also a contract player at MGM and I recommended him for the role. He had a better build and was the dark, swarthy type. Besides who ever heard of a blond Tarzan?

The test went like this: the set was a beautiful clearing in a beautiful jungle with the even more beautiful Joanna Barnes sitting pretty on a log. Along comes Tarzan, dripping wet, and recites the twenty-third Psalm. You read right... the whole thing.

The producers told me that this Tarzan was going to be more intelligent than previous jungle fellas. Right! The twenty-third Psalm has twenty times more words than I eventually said in the whole film. So much for smarts.

At the same time they were testing guys for the role of the ape man, they were testing new and different loincloths. They had ones made out of spotted leopard (imitation), lion (imitation) and the tried and true chamois skin model (not imitation) that had been around since before Johnny Weissmuller.

My favorite was made out of colorful beads sewn on a leather background. It was really different and really uncomfortable. When you sat on a log you would roll off. And when you walked you sounded like Humphry Bogart going from room to room through one of those bead curtains in the Maltese Falcon. Not good for sneaking around in the jungle.

They picked the old fashioned loincloth and me to wear it. The filming was great fun. The film was not. In Gabe Essoe's book, "Tarzan of The Movies," he reviews the film in the chapter headed, "Tarzan The Worst!"

Our film held that title for many years until Bo Derek starred in and produced with her husband, John, the second remake. Their rendition of "Tarzan The Ape Man" is now, "Tarzan The Worst!"

If you're made to watch any of the three versions as some kind of sadistic torture, make it easy on yourself and watch Johnny Weissmuller in the original. Even if it's in brilliant black and white it is, by far, the best of the three. (And it has now been colorized.)

CHAPTER 5
WE STILL CALL HIM COACH

I wish my son, Brad, could have experienced being a member of a winning athletic team. Just being a member of an average team would have been nice.

Sadly, the Pop Warner football team he was on was the responsibility of a guy who was there just to get brownie points at the Savings and Loan he worked for. It's called "Community Service." He was trying to climb that corporate ladder.

Notice I didn't call him coach. He had no knowledge of the game. He was a stranger to fitness, being rounder than the football. I saw him describe an exercise to the 45 kids all in

Coach Wooden with the Miller boys, Denny and Kent.

full gear, pads, even helmets. Not one of the kids could do one rep. That should have given him a clue that the exercise was too hard. Instead, he got angry with them. Then he got down on the ground to show them how to do it and couldn't do one rep without all that stuff on. Then he really got mad at them.

To him, winning wasn't everything, it was the ONLY thing. After four games, the total score was one hundred eighteen for their opponents and six points for them.

Kids were sobbing in the locker room at half time. One kid broke a leg. When I saw this perfect example of "The Peter Principle" slap a kid on his helmet for missing a tackle, it was time, way past time, to make a change. Brad and I decided that almost any other activity would be a healthier way to spend his time. He joined a fitness program and thirty years later, he still works out.

Coach John Wooden, the college basketball coach with the most National Championships to his credit - 10, and one of two men in the Coaching Hall of Fame and the Basketball Players' Hall of Fame (the other being Lenny Wilkens), coached at UCLA for twenty-seven years. My brother Kent and I had the privilege of being coached by him. I so wish my son had had that experience.

> "His most important lesson... that you are a winner, a success, if you do your best... a lesson he hoped would stick with you throughout your life."

"Coach." That's what all his players still call him, was first of all a teacher. His most important lesson... that you are a winner, a success, if you do your best... a lesson he hoped would stick with you throughout your life. Winning had nothing to do with the score of a game. It was all about how well you played and about that great feeling you got when you knew you had done the best that you could do.

Coach called that success. Take a look at his "Pyramid of Success" on page 33. He still gives talks based on it to athletic groups as well as business groups around the country. He is still in great demand as a motivational speaker.

Coach was also a father figure and a leader. He led by example. He was and still is fit at ninety-two - mentally and physically. He is a flash back to the Golden Age of Greece – "A Sound Mind in A Sound Body," in today's language - "An Affirm Mind in A Firm Body." He wasn't macho in a macho world. No four letter words. "Goodness gracious sakes alive!" and you knew he was angry.

He was a poet in the locker room. After all, he had been an English teacher. He was always soft spoken. He was positive even in negative situations.

He was a prince in the gym. The rules of the game were just that, rules, not to be broken or bent. That didn't mean he didn't want you to play hard. If you dove on the hardwood

Three time All-American at Purdue University.

floor for the ball and came up with bloody knees, he'd be there to pat you on the back. If you punched someone in the nose, you'd be sitting next to him on the bench. Help your opponent up if he falls, don't stand over him and taunt him while he's down. Coach always kept the ship afloat – the sportsmanship.

Kent and I played for him at UCLA. Kent, my brother, was by far the most talented. He moved like a six-foot seven-inch cat. He had the grace, the economy of motion, and the control of a dancer. Me? I made the team because I was dating Nancy Wooden, Coach's daughter. He would rather have me sitting next to him on the bench on a Saturday night than next to Nancy anywhere else.

At six-foot four-inches, I could never dunk. I told Coach that I really could but I was afraid of heights. Kent could soar. He was a joy to watch.

We have reunions of coaches and players every other year. At the last one, there were over one hundred fifty players and six coaches. All the coaches had been assistant coaches for Coach John.

What a good feeling being with your teammates again. Lots of laughter, a few joyful tears and bunches of hugs. Athletes are the only men in our society that can hug publicly without a stigma.

Coach is still as witty, humble and loving as he has been all his life. It is always great to hug him.

I proudly belong to three groups of men. The biggest group is those men that have been honorably discharged from the U.S. Army. Belonging to that group has taught me to hate war.

I belong to the P.T.A. — the "Past Tarzans Association." It is a very small group of nineteen men who have played the role of Tarzan on film. That experience taught me not to take myself too seriously. Being a cartoon will do that to you. My Nevada license is — XTARZAN.

But the group of men I'm proudest to be a member of is that bunch of athletes who had the privilege of being coached by John Wooden.

I love you, Coach!

> "Me? I made the team because I was dating Nancy Wooden, Coach's daughter. He would rather have me sitting next to him on the bench on a Saturday night than next to Nancy anywhere else."

JOHN WOODEN'S PYRAMID OF SUCCESS

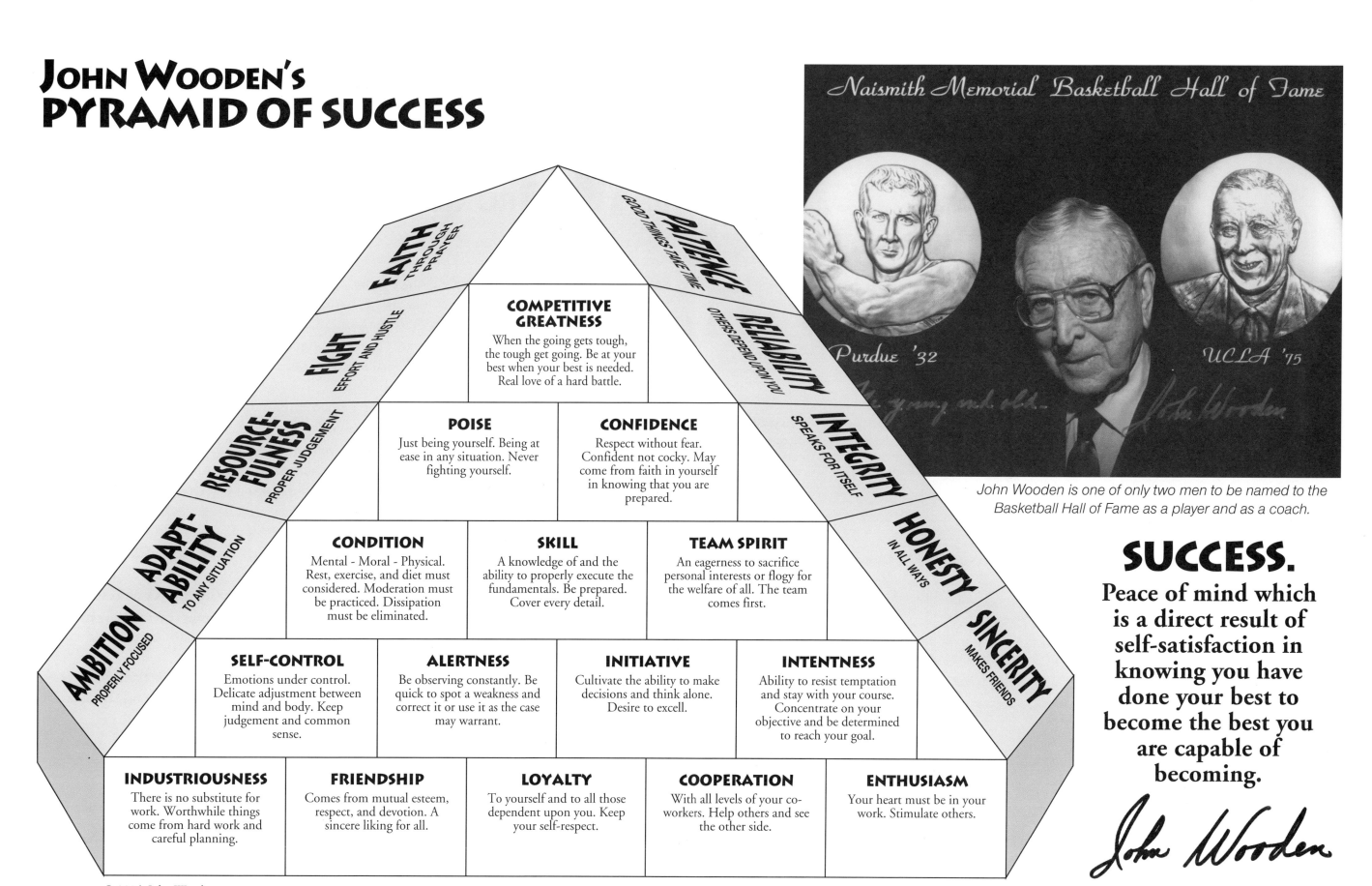

FAITH THROUGH PRAYER

PATIENCE GOOD THINGS TAKE TIME

FIGHT EFFORT AND HUSTLE

RELIABILITY OTHERS DEPEND UPON YOU

RESOURCE-FULNESS PROPER JUDGEMENT

INTEGRITY SPEAKS FOR ITSELF

ADAPT-ABILITY TO ANY SITUATION

HONESTY IN ALL WAYS

AMBITION PROPERLY FOCUSED

SINCERITY MAKES FRIENDS

COMPETITIVE GREATNESS
When the going gets tough, the tough get going. Be at your best when your best is needed. Real love of a hard battle.

POISE
Just being yourself. Being at ease in any situation. Never fighting yourself.

CONFIDENCE
Respect without fear. Confident not cocky. May come from faith in yourself in knowing that you are prepared.

CONDITION
Mental - Moral - Physical. Rest, exercise, and diet must considered. Moderation must be practiced. Dissipation must be eliminated.

SKILL
A knowledge of and the ability to properly execute the fundamentals. Be prepared. Cover every detail.

TEAM SPIRIT
An eagerness to sacrifice personal interests or flogy for the welfare of all. The team comes first.

SELF-CONTROL
Emotions under control. Delicate adjustment between mind and body. Keep judgement and common sense.

ALERTNESS
Be observing constantly. Be quick to spot a weakness and correct it or use it as the case may warrant.

INITIATIVE
Cultivate the ability to make decisions and think alone. Desire to excell.

INTENTNESS
Ability to resist temptation and stay with your course. Concentrate on your objective and be determined to reach your goal.

INDUSTRIOUSNESS
There is no substitute for work. Worthwhile things come from hard work and careful planning.

FRIENDSHIP
Comes from mutual esteem, respect, and devotion. A sincere liking for all.

LOYALTY
To yourself and to all those dependent upon you. Keep your self-respect.

COOPERATION
With all levels of your co-workers. Help others and see the other side.

ENTHUSIASM
Your heart must be in your work. Stimulate others.

© 2004 John Wooden

Naismith Memorial Basketball Hall of Fame

Purdue '32

UCLA '75

John Wooden is one of only two men to be named to the Basketball Hall of Fame as a player and as a coach.

SUCCESS.
Peace of mind which is a direct result of self-satisfaction in knowing you have done your best to become the best you are capable of becoming.

John Wooden

CHAPTER 6
BROKEN DREAMS

At the college level of basketball, I found out my dream would not come true. To be a professional basketball player was, up to that time, an obsession and my only dream. From grade school on, I spent hours practicing and playing. Every home we lived in, Dad built a backboard and rim in the back yard. In Bloomington, Indiana, where I was born; in Silver Spring, Maryland, just outside of Washington, D.C.; in Baldwin, Long Island, New York; and the best one – in Westwood, California.

A friend of mine in Indiana told me he had improved his eye and shooting ability by making the target smaller. So Dad took down the rim and had a welder cut a chunk out of it. We made it fifteen inches in diameter, three inches smaller than the regulation eighteen inches. After thousands of shots, it worked. My shooting percentage improved.

> "I did exercises to improve my vertical jump. White men can't jump. At least this one couldn't."

I practiced in all kinds of weather and at all times of day and night. I did exercises to improve my vertical jump. White men can't jump. At least this one couldn't.

I set up obstacle courses out of furniture in our basement and dribbled the ball back and forth between the tables and chairs, blindfolded.

I loved the game of basketball. My practice paid off. It paid off with a full basketball scholarship to UCLA and the privilege of a lifetime – the chance to be coached by John Wooden.

But my talent, even with the best coaching in the world, wouldn't take me to the next level. The realization hit me in my junior year. Denial is not a river in Egypt. It was the state of mind at the time and for several years after.

But, I've been lucky all my life. The happy accident of a career in film and TV happened. I still enjoy watching basketball. I think the NBA has the best athletes in the world. The most agile, coordinated, enduring, sharpest-eyed... most gifted athletes in history... Nureyevs in sneakers. Among their numbers, and there are very few of them (in the hundreds) Michael

"BE QUICK – BUT DON'T HURRY!"
—Coach John Wooden

Jordan is the most gifted. I still love the game. Want to go shoot a few hoops right now?

Being soaked in sports all my school days it's not surprising that I didn't know who George Cukor was. So, when my agent told me that Mr. Cukor would direct my screen test for a contract with MGM Studios, it was no big deal. I had followed a bouncing ball all my life. Show Biz wasn't even in my peripheral vision.

Joan Elan, an English actress, would be testing with me. We were to do a scene from a successful Broadway comedy, "The Voice of The Turtle." I had never heard of the play or the voice of any turtle. I had caught many turtles sunning themselves on the shore of Lake Tippecanoe during sixteen summers I spent at the lake. We stayed in my grandfather's cottage.

Mr. Cukor and Joan educated me. The title of the play was a metaphor for "Spring," the time for mating, for love. The turtle was a turtledove. His voice was his love call for a mate heard in the spring. Who knew? The subject very seldom came up in a gymnasium.

Mr. Cukor assigned a friend of his, a drama coach, to rehearse with us. Joan didn't need her help. I sure did. We went over the scene again and again, sometimes in Cukor's office at MGM and other times in his home in the Hollywood Hills.

I had never been in a home like it. On our first visit, Joan and I were ushered into a large

I was so skinny, I didn't have a shadow. (Baldwin High School, 1948.)

oval room. The long walls of the oval room were divided in half by facing pocket doors. The butler closed the doors behind us. We were to wait for our coach. For several weeks of rehearsals Mr. Cukor did not join us in his office or at his home. Directing a screen test was way down on his list of priorities.

One half of the oval room had a huge bay window looking out over a swimming pool and onto a formal garden beyond. At the end of the garden, at least one hundred yards away, was a gazebo with a view of Los Angeles, the ocean and on a clear day – Catalina Island.

At the end of the other half of the room was a fireplace bordered by some kind of brass horns. They were about ten feet tall and sitting on their bell ends.

On one wall, I found out later, were museum quality paintings. The only one I recognized was a Klee. I turned to Joan, who had taken a seat by the bay window, and let out a long "Wow" breath, and at the same time I placed my hand on the wall to lean on it.

I jumped back with a start! The wall I had leaned on was covered with padded suede. Surprised? Very! Joan got a giggle out of that. She had lived in a much different world than I had.

The floor was parquet, a mosaic of exotic woods. There wasn't a basketball in sight. Joan and I rehearsed there several times a week for several months. Remember, I am a misplaced basketball player. Joan was an actress and soon wanted to get on with the test. She'd had enough rehearsing.

> "If you don't relax in the next take you can expect that bowl to come flying at your head!"

When the day of the screen test arrived I was almost catatonic. In the past weeks I had learned of Mr. Cukor's track record. The fact that he had directed Katharine Hepburn and Jimmy Stewart in "The Philadelphia Story", Katharine Hepburn and Spencer Tracy in "Pat and Mike" and Rex Harrison and Audrey Hepburn in "My Fair Lady" left me in awe. I kept asking myself "What the hell am I doing here?"

The first shot of the screen test was my entrance into the apartment set. Not more than three steps into the room and Mr. Cukor yelled, "Cut. You see that bowl of waxed fruit on the table?" I nodded yes. "If you don't relax in the next take, you can expect that bowl to come flying at your head!"

That broke the ice. Or should I say the raw fear that bound me – the fear of making a fool of myself – the fear of making a dumb mistake lessened. That's what a director does for an actor. He or she creates an atmosphere on the set that says, "You are among friends here, you can goof up. We are here to help. We know you're not perfect. Let's have some fun. After all, they call it a play."

With the name George Cukor, Director, on the title frame of the test, no one could fail to get a contract, not even an untrained, stumble novice like me. I have thanked Mr. Cukor many times. He has been gone for many years but I thank him again, now.

I almost forgot... My mother and father were invited to Mr. Cukor's home for lunch. Among the other guests that day were Billie Burke and Michael Romanoff. My folks talked about that luncheon for years. Thank you Mr. Cukor. I got to dance with Norma Shearer at a party Mr. Cukor gave for her. Thank you Mr. Cukor.

And thank you Mr. Cukor for a dinner party at Cole Porter's house. Cole Porter was also a "Hoosier." I asked Mr. Porter "What the heck is a Hoosier?" He told me three derivations he had heard for "Hoosier."

There used to be the canals in the northeastern part of Indiana. The barges going up and down the canals were pulled by mules. The men who drove those mules were mostly German and were called "Hussars." "From Hussar to Hoosier was a long reach," Cole told us.

Back when Indiana was on the frontier, many people lived in isolated cabins. Indiana was named because it was the home of many Indians. So, before you answered a knock at your locked door you would yell, "Who-is-yer?" Mr. Porter thought this the most likely of the three derivations, but he liked the third one the best.

He said it was not unusual, after a bar room brawl, back when there was no shortage of brawlers in Indiana, for one of the fighters to untangle himself from the mangled mob on the floor and yell, "Who's ear?"

It doesn't matter to me that "Hoosier" is still a mystery. What really matters to me is that I thank you, Mr. George Cukor for all your joyful generosity!

CHAPTER 7
I PLAYED AGAINST MICHAEL JORDAN

UCLA and North Carolina have had two of the winningest college basketball programs over the past forty-five years. Coach John Wooden and Coach Dean Smith have been the reasons for their success.

How about a game between the alumni players from UCLA versus the N.C. alumni? What a great idea to raise money for charity. So it was arranged.

There have been many graduates from each school who went on to have good careers in the NBA. Some of the players were among the best ever to play the game. A few are still playing.

I was thrilled to be included on the UCLA roster. It wasn't because of my basketball talent. I was the oldest alum, sort of a curiosity, a basketball dinosaur. I shared locker room space with Reggie Miller, who greeted me with, "Nice to meet you sir." My gray beard and weather-beaten face command respect, or maybe "sympathy" would be a more appropriate word.

Reggie Miller was – is one of the best three-point shooters in the history of the three-point shot. He's always been a clutch player, the one to give the ball to in the last seconds of the game when it's your last chance to come from behind. He's the guy who wants the ball, a guy who has ice water in his veins. A guy who has won many games

> "From our bench, Bill Walton bellowed, 'If you don't take a two-hander, you haven't got a hair on your fanny!' Once a poet, always a poet."

in the last second with a three-point shot you would bet your last dollar hasn't a chance in a million of going in.

The team made its entrance onto the court. There weren't many empty seats. The charity would be pleased. There must have been 15,000 to 16,000 fans. We went into the usual lay-up line and that's when I noticed my legs were made of rubber. Not to worry. There was no chance I'd do anything but sit on the bench. Reggie wasn't the only pro on the team.

Ten minutes into the game I noticed a few other guys seemed to have rubber legs too. But most of the guys were in great youth... I mean shape. The size of the players surprised me. I hadn't watched a basketball game from a floor level seat in thirty years. These fellas were much taller and broader than the ones I'd played with back in the fifties. There was hardly enough room on the court for them. Watching the games on TV is deceptive. The younger the players, the bigger they were. They'll have to widen and lengthen the court soon.

A time out was called. Who knows why? We were all busy yakking on the bench. Catching up with a few old teammates was more important than the game. Everyone gathered around Coach John, but the yakking continued. Coach said, "You don't have to stop talking but just look at me. The fans will think you're listening to me." I don't think he said anything after that. I heard Bill Walton a lot.

What was that? My name? Uh-oh! Dribbling down the court I remember several guys passing me like I was standing still. Maybe I was. I was trying to find Reggie. He was by far our best player. I'd pass it to him. From our bench, Bill Walton bellowed, "If you don't take a two-hander, you haven't got a hair on your fanny!" Once a poet, always a poet.

No one, I repeat, no one in basketball had shot the ball two handed since the early fifties. That had been the way I shot. I told you I was a dinosaur. Why not... I took a two-hander and it rattled the backboard without touching the rim. I had the touch of a jackhammer operator. I could hear Walton's laugh.

I was winded. After all I had been up and down the court twice. Reggie took a shot next time down and North Carolina got the rebound. Here comes a fast break, two on one. I was the one. I was backing up a fast as I could. On my right, dribbling the ball was Michael Jordan and on my left was James Worthy.

I calmly stopped, stepped forward as they streaked by me. I cupped my hands and yelled to the thousands — "HELP!"

To this day I don't know which one of them dunked the ball. I could tell one of them did because I could hear it rip through the net. I will be able to tell my grandchildren that I played against two of the best basketball players who ever played the game. I may leave a few of the details out, but you can be sure I'll tell them. I've already told everybody else.

Chucks Connors played professionally in both basketball and baseball.

CHAPTER 8
CHUCK CONNERS

A PRO IN BASEBALL, BASKETBALL AND ACTING

Chuck Conners was a great athlete. Very few men in the history of sport have been talented enough to play at the professional level in two sports. Chuck was one. He played basketball for the Boston Celtics and baseball for the Brooklyn Dodgers.

Many actors were athletes before their Movie/TV careers. John Wayne played football, as did Ward Bond. Dennis Weaver was a hurdler. Rafer Johnson was a decathlete. Alex Karas was a pro football player before he knocked out his horse in "Blazing Saddles." He also starred with his wife in their own TV series, "Webster," and served as announcer on Monday Night Football.

Frank Gifford was on Monday Night Football for over twenty years and "Dandy" Don Meredith was there with him for part of that time. They had both been pro football players. Tom Selleck played basketball and volleyball for University of Southern California. Johnny Weissmuller and Buster Crabbe were Olympic swimmers. Arnold Schwarzenegger played soccer before his "body building days." There were many other "jocks" that became successful in film.

See, acting is a team sport. Sports and acting use the same terms. In a *PLAY*, on stage or on a court, there are stars and supporting actors. There are role players in theater and sport. Both practice/rehearse. Both have fans. Both have coaches/directors. The moving picture can be on film or on a field. An actor can carry a play; so can a halfback.

Teamwork is the foundation for both disciplines. Even if an actor is doing a monologue, it won't be a winner if the actor and the guy working the spotlight aren't teammates. Not many in the audience can see you in the dark.

The *MOVING* picture is the attraction. Actors or athletes in action, whether it's the quarterback saying, "Hut-hut" or the director saying, "Action" - that's when things get interesting.

That's why actors train their bodies, keeping them strong, limber and agile, so they can get their bodies to do an action on call. Actors and athletes are *NOW artists*. Not like sculptors or writers or painters who can do their art anytime. Actors and athletes have to do their creating NOW. The show starts at eight. Game time is at three. The director says action —

act NOW.

Athletes already have trained bodies. They have control of their movements. They move – no, they glide with economy of motion. Smooth like a dancer. So it's just a short step from playing on a field to playing on a stage. And, like me, they all enjoy the give and take of a team effort. They like sharing the responsibility of carrying a play as its star or in a supporting role.

Chuck Conners was one of these athlete/actors. He always played active roles. Playing a man... a confident man... an action hero. He was about six-feet seven-inches tall and over two hundred pounds and lean. He played cowmen, not boys. He played Indians and he played "The Rifleman."

"The Rifleman" was one of twenty-six Western TV shows each week. That's right, it was the peak of Western shows on the box. Twenty-six minutes of the past out West in a half hour show minus the advertisements. Most shows shot thirty-nine episodes for the year. If you were lucky enough to have a running part in an hour show, you worked most of the year. "Rifleman", "The Deputy" with Henry Fonda and "Have Gun Will Travel" with Richard Boone, were all half-hour westerns.

When I was working on "Rifleman," I had a scene to do with Chuck in the dirt street outside the town's general store. I was playing the part of a cowboy known for his strength. Chuck and his stage son were loading supplies from the store onto their wagon. Sacks of potatoes and flour, beef jerky – I asked if I could help, bragging that I was really strong.

In fact, I said going over to Chuck's horse and crouching down and putting my arms under the horse's belly, "I can lift your horse. Wanna see me do it?" Chuck says, "That won't be necessary!" They finished loading, got on the wagon, a slap of the reins and they rode off. A couple of more rehearsals and we're all ready to shoot the scene.

"Action." We start the scene. It is going well. We get to the part where I say, "I can lift your horse. Wanna see me do it?"

Chuck folds his arms and says, "Yep, I'd like to see you do that!" Leaving me holding the nag. He roared – Chuck, not the horse, ran in a circle and off the set where two of his baseball teammates were cracking up. Mr. Conners was having fun. He loved working, but there was always time for a relaxing chuckle.

Forty years later we worked together on a TV show called "Werewolf." He was playing the "Werewolf" and I was a German fisherman. We worked nights in a thick fog down by San Pedro Harbor. His back hurt from years of doing fight scenes and he sat down between takes to rest his knees. I hate it when my film heroes get old. But Chuck still had the gift of laughter. You could hear it through the fog.

CHAPTER 9
RAFER JOHNSON

AT THE TOP OF THE PYRAMID

"Fortius, Altius, Citius," (stronger, higher, swifter)" - these are the goals of the Olympic athletes. The Olympic Games were started in 776 B.C. and were held on the plains of Olympia, Greece, every four years until 393 A.D.

They were held as a break from war. They were a temporary festival of peace and included athletic games and contests of choral poetry and dance.

After a short break of 1,502 years, the Olympic Games were revived in 1896, in Greece, and again held every four years. A guy named Pierre de Fredy, Baron de Coubertin came up with the idea. Since it was his idea, he was the natural choice to be President of the International Olympic Committee for the next thirty-one years.

Of all the athletes, and there are thousands that compete in all the sports, the decathlete is considered to be the best of the best. He is certainly the most versatile.

Ten events are held over two consecutive days. They are always held in the same order: day one – the hundred meters, long jump, shot put, high jump and the 400 meters; day two – 110 meter hurdles, discus throw, pole vault, javelin and the 1,500 meters complete the competition.

Rafer Johnson won a silver medal in the 1956 Olympics and a gold medal in 1960. In 1960, it came down to the last event, the 1,500-meter race, to decide who would take the gold. It was between C.K. Yang and Rafer.

This was an unusual situation, very unusual. The two men attended the same school, UCLA. They were coached by the same man, Ducky Drake, and they were best

Rafer Johnson at the Special Olympics.

43

Rafer Johnson carries the Olympic torch.

friends. Can you imagine what a thin line Ducky had to walk? That doesn't give his position enough credit. He had trained the two best athletes in the world at the same time on the same track and field and still held the trust and love of both men.

It was a win, win, win situation. Rafer got gold. C.K. won the 1,500 meter event but not by enough seconds to win the gold. It was such a close finish that the Italian crowd chanted "Give them both a gold medal, give them both a gold medal..." Ducky was right with both of them.

Fifty years later Rafer is still a winner, a special winner. He's the Chairman of the Board of Governors for the Special Olympics. He's been involved since its beginnings.

Ever been to a Special Olympics? Go! And take a box or two of Kleenex. You won't cry tears of sadness. You'll bubble over at the sight of so much beauty, so much love.

> **"Then it happened— all the runners stopped. They turned around, went back and helped their buddy up."**

At a Special Olympics held several years ago, the athletes were at their starting marks for a race. The distance of the race is irrelevant. The starter's gun went off and the race began. About halfway through, one contestant fell. First one and then another and then all the other runners looked back and saw their fallen friend.

Then it happened — all the runners stopped. They turned around, went back and helped their buddy up. Then they all joined hands and walked together across the finish line. Here — want some of my Kleenex?

I'm proud to be one of Rafer's many friends. We were teammates on the UCLA Basketball team. I voted for him along with all those friends for student body president. But now, he makes me mad. Why? I'll tell you why!

He's in his late sixties. So am I. He doesn't have a gray hair on his head. My whole head is gray – beard, hair and face. He still looks like he did accepting his Gold Medal in 1960.

Remember the story "The Portrait of Dorian Gray?" Rafer's "Dorian Black." We all get older and he stays young. Unlike Dorian Gray his portrait doesn't even age. He has no secret formula. What he has is his son who is his personal trainer. They work out together five times a week at 6 A.M.

The U.S. leads the world in overweight people. If you want to get in shape and you're looking for a role model, Rafer is the best I know of. Exercise to live, not live to exercise. That is a lesson for us all. It's work, but it works.

The 2004 Olympics are just around the corner. Don't be surprised to hear Rafer's name called. He'll be in the same size sweat suit he wore in 1960.

CHAPTER 10
TOM SELLECK... A STAR

"Higgins." John Hillerman created the character on Magnum P.I. Millions of fans watched as he stuck barbs in Tom Selleck week after week. John had a barb sticking in him the morning we worked together. John was in the next make-up chair and he wasn't happy.

At that time, Honolulu had several towering condominium buildings. The higher your condo, the more spectacular the view from your home. John had the penthouse in one of these buildings and clouds and mountains were his neighbors. A real chunk of heaven.

I listened to his problem. I couldn't help but hear him. He was less than three feet from me and having make-up applied is not a noisy event.

It seems that John was having his heaven remodeled. Big time. Walls were being torn down and moved to enlarge rooms, that sort of thing.

He had been on the mainland making personal appearances and had a few days wait till the next one, so he decided to fly home and check out the changes being made. Good thing he did.

He found very little progress had been made and what had been done was wrong. Very wrong. A wall had been built where no wall should be.

The make-up people had to back off for a moment. It's not good to apply eye make-up when your hand is shaking from laughter.

The remodeling had been going on for over a year at this point. Instead of yelling at the foreman, John said he took him gently by the arm and guided him to a window that looked out on a thirty-five-story building two blocks away.

"When you started this job," he quietly told the man, "that building wasn't there!"

That morning was the most fun I've ever had in a make-up chair. Off stage John doesn't sound like his character Higgins. John's from Texas. He doesn't sound like that either. John is a very good actor. Not only that, he has many other talents. One of them was hosting, on and off

John Hillerman

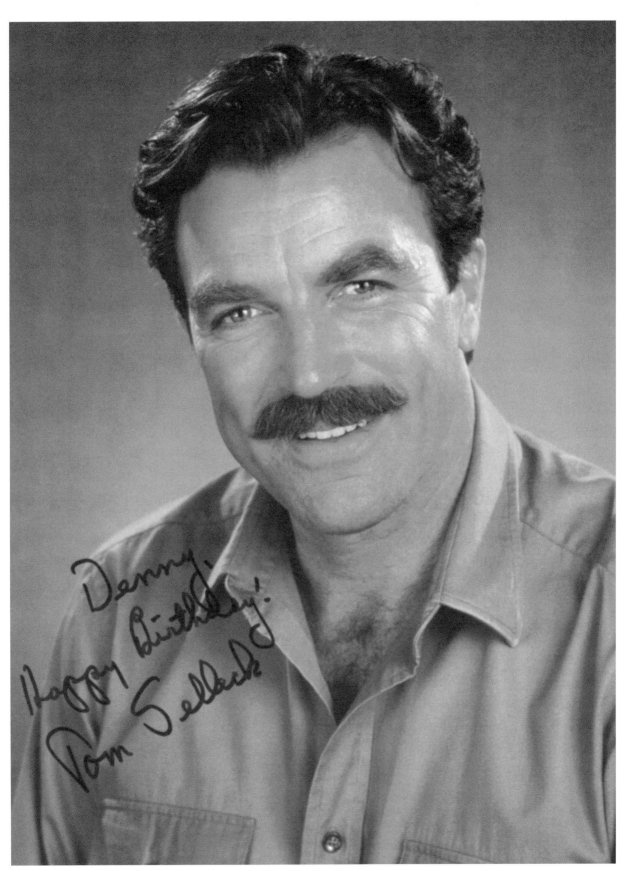

Tom Selleck – A real star.

camera, for a parade. That's hard to do. For two hours or sometimes three, the host has the responsibility to keep the parade moving even when it's standing still. Three hours of ad lib is tough. John does it better than anyone. He's witty, informative and funny. He is far better than any parade. If you see John Hillerman is hosting a parade, any parade… don't miss it.

If you're an actor and get a chance to work with Tom Selleck, jump at it. I worked with him three times on Magnum PI. Being in Hawaii is pretty nice duty. Working there is even better. Working with Tom tops it off.

He's relaxed and generous. That means he's easy to work with; as easy as it gets. And he is a Star. When the company was on location, it would be on the far side of the island. Tom was working that day and full tour busses were always parked nearby. Hundreds of fans poured out waiting for a glimpse. When Tom wasn't working, there was not a fan or bus in sight.

It was about time for the summer Olympics on my first Magnum job. Tom had put together a poster of himself in the U.S. Olympic volleyball uniform. The posters were in every store window in Honolulu. All the proceeds went to support the Olympic team. Tom was a volleyball player at the University of Southern California.

He also played basketball at USC. I saw him on a TV talk show telling about his basketball experience at USC. He said, "Every time I went into the game there was a huge ovation!"

> **"When you started this job,"** he quietly told the man, **"that building wasn't there!"**

I thought to myself, that's not like Tom to boast like that. Then he said, "Did I forget to mention that I was substituting for our "All American Center"?

One of the parts I played on Magnum was that of a down and almost out ex-marine. My daughter was played by Shannon Doherty. This marine had been a member of a special combat unit and he had a tattoo on his arm to tell the world that he was proud of that fact. The make-up man took over an hour each day to apply it on my forearm.

One day the company was shooting in a dingy smoke-filled bar in Pearl Harbor. I was leaning against a wall across the street waiting to work.

"I can put a beautiful American Eagle on that," came a voice at my side. I turned to see a guy, arms covered with tattoos, pointing at the phony tattoo on my arm.

I had been standing in front of his tattoo parlor.

"Thanks, maybe later. I have to work right now."

I crossed the street and went into the bar. When I told the make-up man what had happened, I swear I could see him grow four-inches taller.

 # CHAPTER 11
GET REAL!

Yesterday I was getting my thirty minutes of aerobics on our semi-recumbent exercycle and surfing through the TV channels for some athletic event, i.e., a basketball game or a marathon race so I could pretend I was one of the competitors. At my age I need all the help I can get to keep peddling, and watching a group of young athletes compete reminds me of my youth and gives me a boot in the rear.

I happen to click on an infomercial for some new miracle fitness machine. The perky person taking up most of the TV screen promised that using this machine, (only three payments of $29.95), for four minutes a day, three times a week, will make a new person out of me in just eight days.

I have a degree from UCLA in kinesiology (fancy name for physical education). I used to be a personal fitness trainer and I don't see how a company can get away with telling lies like that. Becoming physically fit takes much more time, much more exercise over a much longer period of time (months not days) and we have to do a lot of different exercises to strengthen all our muscle groups, not just our inner thighs or our butt.

But that wasn't what really got my attention. Perky person said, "You can believe what I'm telling you because I'm a REAL person, not a model or an actor!"

Now I know those weren't her words. Some infomercial scriptwriter strung that thought out on paper. By the way, in a recent survey of one million fourth, fifth and sixth graders, they were asked, "What do you want to be when you grow up?" 738,244 kids said, "I want to be an infomercial scriptwriter!" Right!

The following list might be of interest to this infomercial scriptwriter and Perky Person.

The following actors have raised and donated hundreds of millions of dollars to a huge variety of charities:

Mary Tyler Moore   The National Diabetes Association
Jerry Lewis   Muscular Dystrophy
Danny Kaye and Katie Couric   UNICEF
Danny Thomas   St. Jude's Hospital
Spencer Tracy   John Tracy Clinic for Deaf Children

Oprah Winfrey	Numerous charities
Paul Newman	The Paul Newman Foundation
John Ritter	Cerebral Palsy
Sally Struthers	Save The Children
Carroll O'Connor	Anti-drug programs
Mariette Hartley	MADD
Carol Burnett	Anti-drug programs
Rafer Johnson	The Special Olympics
Robert Redford	Sundance Institute; environmental issues
Gov. Arnold Schwartzenegger	The President's Council on Fitness
Betty White	Animal rights
Emma Samms	Make A Wish Foundation
Billy Crystal, Whoopi Goldberg and Robin Williams	Comic Relief
Julia Roberts and George Clooney	The 911 Fund

The list could go on. There are thousands of involved actors, but you "Perky Person" and esteemed infomercial scriptwriter, get the point. Or maybe not.

If you think you are more sensitive, more giving, more caring, more generous, more charitable or a more concerned citizen than any of these actors — **GET REAL!**

CHAPTER 12
SAMMY DAVIS COULD DO ANYTHING

A letter is a gift from a very shy friend. Garrison Keillor wrote that and I believe him.

A fan letter is delayed applause. Film and TV actors do their acting without an audience. The crew has a job to do so they aren't watching. Sir Lawrence Olivier said, "In television wherever an actor goes to rehearse, there'll be a guy with a hammer."

You won't hear applause on a sound stage. Maybe if you finish the last scene in the show and everyone can go home, or when a dangerous stunt is done and no one gets hurt, or when someone like Sir Lawrence does a three-page monologue – a little applause will happen. It's the same for athletes and dancers and singers – all entertainers. The fans may have been thousands of miles away from your performance and they want to tell you how much they enjoyed seeing the film of you when you scored a run or your dance leap, or the way you sang their favorite song.

A fan asking for your autograph is a handshake on paper. "I'd like to have something that your hand touched to remind me of how your performance touched me. If you can sign a photo of yourself, I can remember those moments more vividly." That is a definite "thank you."

The word "fan" comes from "fanatic". When I see film of the screaming, crying, clamoring teenage girls being held back from burying Elvis Presley, Frank Sinatra, Brad Pitt or Joe Namath, the word FANATIC fits. But most fans have a brain and a heart and come bearing gifts.

The fans I appreciate most are the ones who do the same work, fellow actors. When I was an athlete, compliments — praise from a teammate really pumped me up. The same good feeling happens when an actor tells me, "You did a good job." It is also a high for me when I congratulate another jock or actor.

I was watching a TV special called "I Am A Dancer," about the life of Rudolf Nureyev. I was watching it with Juliet Prowse, one of the most successful dancers in the world. Her life's dream was to be a ballerina, but she was too tall. On point she towered over the other dancers.

At the end of the show, Nureyev performed a soaring leap and did the splits in mid-air. The producers froze the frame and ran the credits over the image of the leap. Juliet jumped

A "Sam" of many talents!

out of her seat like a kid at a circus. She yelled with a knowing joy, "Look, that leap is sensational!" She was a dancer thrilled by the performance of another dancer.

Sammy Davis was one of the most talented men to ever step on a stage. He could sing, dance, do impersonations, and he could tell jokes with the best comedians.

I've seen and known some fast draws. I wasn't bad at pulling a six-shooter out of my holster in a hurry. Sammy made my draw look like slow motion. He was the fastest I ever saw. And twirl a gun? He could twirl two guns, forwards and backwards, above his head, at his hips and holster them and re-draw while singing a song. John Wayne would have been proud to be half as fast.

Sammy performed everywhere to packed houses. This night he was on stage in Tahoe. He came out and sang several songs, told a few jokes and then changed his pace and got serious for a moment.

Danny Kaye was seated above and behind me. Sammy started by saying, "There is a man in the audience I want to thank," and went on to say what a great actor this man was and on and on. I turned in my seat to applaud Mr. Kaye and get a look at this world-famous entertainer and UNICEF worker. Then I heard my name! Sammy had been giving me the honors.

I stood, weak in the knees and bowed my head to Sammy. I sat down rather quickly. Not because I wanted to but because my knees gave out. The reason for his praise was this... he had seen an episode of "Wagon Train" called, "Charlie Shut Up," starring Dick York, a fine character actor. Charlie was an Indian. My character, Duke Shannon had broken his leg and was snowed in by a blizzard. Two men start out as enemies and end up friends, helping each other survive. When Charlie is accidentally killed, I got to say a monologue holding the dying Indian in my arms, sobbing all the while; showing a white man's love for his friend, a red man. Thank you Norman Jolley for writing those beautiful thoughts.

A few times in my acting career I have had the privilege of saying the lines of a writer, a writer much wiser than I, that tell of the human condition and the love that we can feel for others, even when those others had once been enemies. This was one of those scripts.

Because Sammy had experienced that breach between people of different color all of his life, the TV story had special meaning for him. I was invited to a party he gave after his performance, and I thanked him for his generous introduction. He was a most gracious host and I will always remember with pride his appreciation of my work. It was really Norman Jolley's work.

Sammy Davis was a tiny, short, bowlegged, ugly, one-eyed, black Jew. To me, and millions of others he was beautiful, inside and out.

CHAPTER 13
MAC THE NICE

The Hollywood Hackers were a group of men, mostly actors and a few producers, a couple of directors and one or two stunt men. We got together once a month to play golf. We'd play at a different course each time and sometimes those among us that had a talent—singing, joke telling – would put on a little show for the locals. The money raised would go to a local charity.

A perfect Will Rogers.

It was at one of these events that I first met Mac Davis. Mac was one of the most talented guys in Hollywood. For that matter most talented guy anywhere. He wrote songs. He acted. He starred in "North Dallas 40" with Nick Nolte. Sang, danced, played the spoons and was a huge hit playing Will Rogers in the musical of the same name on Broadway. Mac had his own TV variety show and on top of that was, still is, a funny, friendly, full of fun character.

Three of us Hollywood hackers were standing on the first tee at the Cottonwood golf course. The Hackers were divided into groups according to their golfing ability. I was in the clown group. I was an eighteen handicap. Still am. I prided myself as being a better than average athlete. But when it came to golf I was, and still am, a motor moron. I couldn't remember what I did right when I hit a good shot. So good shots didn't happen very often.

Anyway we were about to tee off when we heard laughter from the direction of the clubhouse. Here comes Mac lugging his clubs and laughing. I don't mean giggling. I don't mean chuckling. I don't mean snickering. I mean gut wrenching, out of breath, inner aerobics, out of control laughing.

We shook hands, introductions all around and in no time, all four of us were bubbling over—laughter's like that, contagious.

When Mac finally caught his breath he told us why he was in the condition he was in. He told us he'd been sitting in a booth in the men's room in the clubhouse. He heard a hand slapping metal and looked down and there it was. The guy in the next stall was reaching down and curling his hand up on Mac's side of the partition. A voice joined the slapping "Got any paper over there?" "No," Mac replied, "but I got five ones for a five!"

I hit my drive into a lake.

CHAPTER 14
BETTE-NOT-SO-NICE

Waiting to do a scene for a TV show or a movie has always been hard for me. Even though I've prepared, learned my lines, had the make-up put on and am in the thought out costume, the little demons start gnawing on my mind.

Is it, "John or Jack that's coming to stab or shoot you?" Can I get on the horse before the darn critter takes off down the road? Gotta get it right the first take or he'll spook and I'll never get in the saddle.

Does the make-up hide my cold sore? Are the blanks in my six shooter full load or just a quarter?

Doubt piles on doubt until I'm looking for the EXIT sign. After forty-five years, two hundred thirty-six TV episodes, nineteen feature films and over two hundred TV commercials, I still get a case of the nerves before every shot. Maybe that's okay.

Bette Davis, when asked if she still got nervous before she was called for her close up answered, "If you don't get nervous, get out of the business!"

Actors are like athletes. They get up for the game. Like the book title goes, "Feel the Fear and Do It Anyway." Be gutsy; use the fear. Steven Spielberg says, "Acting is all about courage, the courage to make mistakes, to look foolish, and never give up. Keep on trying."

> **"She turned without saying her line, walked to the director, and said, loud enough for everyone to hear, 'Is he going to say it THAT way?'"**

The wait I have in mind was to do a scene on "Wagon Train" with Ms. Bette Davis. She was playing the part of a frisky woman who owned a bevy of dance hall gals on their way to San Francisco. Just before we were to start our scene, Ms. Davis came out of her dressing room walked to the phony campfire and sat down on a log.

She pulled up her frilly dress, way up, and straightened her silk stockings. I had seen most of her movies and couldn't remember seeing her legs. I would have remembered. They were dancers' legs; long, lithe, lovely. She had the attention of everyone on the set. And my demons were jumping up and down – "How can you remember your lines now?" they screamed.

Virgil Vogel, the director, called for a rehearsal. So, Ms. Davis and I took our places facing each other, next to a Conestoga wagon. "Action!" shouted Vogel. I don't remember what my line was. I do remember what she did after I said it. She stared at me with those Bette Davis eyes. It felt like the longest moment of my life. But it wasn't. The next moment was. She turned without saying her line, walked to the director, and said, loud enough for everyone to hear, "Is he going to say it THAT way?"

Virgil, almost as stunned as I was, said meekly, "Well, yes; that's his character in the show." I played a shy cowboy who was more comfortable talking to his horse than to a woman.

She whirled around, strode back to her mark and barked, "Give it to me again!" By now I was a six-foot four-inch puddle of sweat, but I managed to get my line out. I don't remember anything about how the rest of the scene went. I was mad and just plain numb. When it was over, I was as relieved as I am when leaving the dentist's chair after a root canal.

The next day I saw something I had never seen before. In all the years I had known John McIntyre, I had never seen him mad. He was the kindest, most easy-going man I ever knew. Not that day. Pacing back and forth, fists clinched, breathing hard, really mad. Nobody went near him because no one had ever seen him like that. We didn't know what had made him so irate but we knew who had... it was the "Witch From Hell, Queen Bette". She had struck again!

John McIntyre, Michael Burns and What's His Name.

CHAPTER 15
GO EAST YOUNG WEST, GO EAST

Barnaby West was the name of the last recurring role to be added to the "Wagon Train" cast. The young actor Michael Burns was the perfect choice for the part. Barnaby was a good sixteen-year old kid searching the frontier for his father. Mike played the role for over two years, clear through the last episode of "Wagon Train."

Wagon Train scripts were based on the stories of the pioneers and the history of their westward expansion of the United States. Each television season the train of covered wagons rolled west from St. Louis and ended in San Francisco. Mike, as Barnaby, played his part in the telling of these historical stories.

While writing this book, the memory of Mike kept popping into my mind so I tracked him down. It had only been about forty years since we had talked and Mike had gone East. When we finally connected the first thing Mike said was, "When did you change your name from Scott to Denny?" We got a chuckle out of that.

We relived the Virginia City parade and other cowboy adventures. We found that we both held fond memories of our "getty-up-whoa days." It's so easy to renew old friendships and such a good feeling.

I mentioned our conversation to Candace Rich. Candace has a "Wagon Train" website and is also my webmaster. She knows everything about the fifties. She has another website called Candace@fifties.com. She e-mailed me what Mike had been up to over the past forty years. Mike had been too modest to mention any of his accomplishments.

John McIntyre, Michael Burns and Bob Fuller.

Terry Wilson and Michael Burns.

During that time, he had earned his PhD in history at Yale. He had taught at Yale and in Paris. He had written several award-winning history books, taught history twenty-two years at Mount Holyoke College and retired Emeritus.

He and his wife, Elizabeth Topham Kennan (past President of Mount Holyoke) have retired and moved to a 540-acre cattle and thoroughbred horse farm, and the two of them had recently completed restoration of the farm's main house. Their work on the house received Kentucky's annual Preservation Award for Historic Restoration.

For over forty years, Mike has given thousands of people clear views of history as an actor, a teacher, a builder and as a writer. Mike the actor showed us the U.S. westward migration during the 1850's. Mike the writer told us about a part of French History in his award winning book, "France and the Dreyfus Affair: A Documentary History." Mike the teacher taught modern and contemporary European civilization for twenty- two years at Mount Holyoke. His lectures were described, by a fellow professor, as being "like listening to Demosthenes." And with his wife, Mike the builder helped restore their home to its original historical state.

How fitting. How right is that? Mike and his wife live in a home right out of history.

The title of his latest book is, "This Side of Paradise: A Global History of 1900 – 1950'" published in W.W. Norton's Global Century series. It will be out sometime this year.

Who said, "If we forget history we're bound to repeat it?" Must have been some cowboy that went East.

Michael Burns — actor, professor, writer, historian.

CHAPTER 16
FOUR OSCARS, TWELVE NOMINATIONS

Katharine Hepburn is my idea of a perfect woman. She was a redhead. My mother was a redhead. I married a redhead. Kate was the spunky type; athletic, in a time when women were supposed to be reserved, fragile creatures. She was a tomboy.

I was in love with her from afar, far back in the dark movie theater. The last row, if there was an empty seat. She reminded me of a butterfly in sneakers. A butterfly so strong she could pull you out of your seat and into the dream world she was in.

My brother Kent drove our old Ford north along the Pacific Coast Highway, past Santa Monica, past Malibu to Trancus. Both of us were college athletes. We were fortunate to be playing basketball for Coach John Wooden at UCLA. We had an appointment to have our photos taken on the beach. I was going to use the photographs on TV commercial interviews. No big deal.

The reason we were both quiet, on edge, was that the beach we were going to was Katharine Hepburn's. The meeting had been arranged by the photographer George Hoyningen-Huene, who was a friend of hers. What's more, she was going to be there and fix us lunch.

I knocked on the screen door and we fidgeted while we waited. In less than a minute or was it a second, there she was, smiling in a knit bathing suit. Kent and I mumbled hellos as she pushed the screen open and gave us a greeting worthy of old friends.

"Do you know where I slept last night?" she asked. Before we could answer she said, "Right there on the board floor of the porch. Beds are overrated, don't you think?" How do you answer that?

The next couple of hours are still a vivid dream but one moment in that dream was a nightmare.

Lunch was good – cold chicken, hard-boiled eggs, celery sticks, no dessert. A lunch you would expect for a woman in her fifties that could still wear a knit bathing suit and look twenty. The spice for the lunch was in the conversation between Kate and George. "Winnie said" and "Marlon hid back stage" and "Spence gave me these beads." They spoke of Winston Churchill and Marlon Brando and Spencer Tracy like we would our Aunt Minnie and old buddy Jim. Why not – Winnie and Marlon and Spencer were their friends. Kent and I just ate and soaked this new world in.

On the beach in front of her house, George took some pictures. Kate had joined us. I get a kick out of calling her Kate. She amused herself by trying to skip flat rocks on the ocean.

During a break while George reloaded his cameras, Kate yelled, "Do you boys body surf?" We told her yes. "Teach me!" she said. It was more of an order than a request.

Kent and I looked at the surf, which was breaking into an inch of water, not a good type of wave to surf on. We told her, but she insisted and we obeyed. How could we not obey? By now she had become our queen.

We explained the few simple rules of body surfing and then Kent and I each took a hand and the three of us marched in to a spot just beyond the breakers. We were just chest deep because the waves were breaking right on the shoreline.

I asked her to please change her mind. The surf was not good for riding. Her answer – she let go of our hands, bent over with her hands together pointing toward the shore and let the next wave push her forward. All we saw was her feet flipping over her fanny as the wave drove her face first into the sand.

As we raced to pull her upright I could see the headlines in the newspaper, KATHARINE HEPBURN BREAKS HER NECK –Two idiot surfers held responsible.

She came up spitting sand and trying to get the sand out of that knit bathing suit.

"I must have done something terribly wrong. Let's try again," she said.

Kent and I picked her up and put her down on the beach. She was fine. I was a nervous, boneless blob.

> "Do you know where I slept last night?" she asked. Before we could answer she said, "Right there on the board floor of the porch. Beds are overrated, don't you think?'"

Much to her disappointment the surfing lesson was over.

I still love her forty-five years later. I watch her movies over and over. She is my favorite actress. I thank God we didn't break her neck that day.

Did I mention she was wearing a knit bathing suit?

CHAPTER 17
CABO BLANCO AND CHARLES

Los Angeles de Locos. I don't mean the L.A. that everyone east of Boston thinks of as a wasteland, (East Coast residents don't know that more books are sold in this part of the country than in any part of the U.S.). The Place of The Crazy Angeles I mean is a big chunk of heaven just north of Manzanillo on the west coast of Mexico.

Here the green jungle and the blue Pacific join hands to create the Bay of Tenacitita, a safe haven for yachts and their adventuresome owners on their way south to the Panama Canal or north to Acapulco and the coast of California.

On the edge of the cliffs facing the sunsets sit four two-story buildings. Red tile roofs cover three condos in each structure, one on the ground floor, two above. Each room opens onto a common living room, fifty feet wide, thirty feet deep and a forty-five foot high-beamed ceiling above. This room only has three walls. It's open to the sea. My room, which will be home for ninety-two days, is on the second floor. From my shuttered balcony I can see the cliffs below, the whole bay and the sea beyond. The sound of the surf, four hundred feet below, fills the room. How can anybody be happy in a place like this?

The dining room, in case you don't want room service, is under a seventy-five foot high Palapa. Its cone-shaped roof of palm fronds, supported by twenty-foot palm trunks stripped of their bark, is built in three sections. About every twenty feet there is a space that goes all around the cone. This

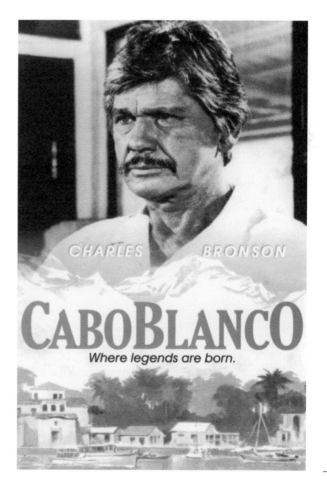

CHARLES BRONSON

CABOBLANCO
Where legends are born.

61

space is just wide enough to let the wind blow through but not let the rain drops in. From a distance a palapa looks like an upside down ice-cream cone. They come in all sizes. This one is huge. A round swimming pool shines near by. It's huge, too.

For three months, Charles Bronson, Jason Robards, Fernando Rey (of "French Connection" fame), Gilbert Roland, Camilla Sparv, Simon MacCorkindale, Dominique Sanda, and I would make a very forgettable movie called "Cabo Blanco".

Notice that the actors are representatives of almost every country in the world. That's called "marketing distribution". In Spain folks will pay to see Fernando, England – Simon, etc. At that time people bought tickets to watch Charles Bronson all over the world. For many years he was the biggest box office attraction in all three of the world's biggest movie markets: Europe, Asia and the U.S.

In such beautiful surroundings there couldn't be any problems. Wrong! Most of them were called Charles. He was unhappy with the script. This is not an unusual concern. Big names want to make the best movie possible. Once you're up there you want to stay there. But Charles would wait until it was time to shoot the scene and then suggest changes. This slowed down everything so the writers were brought on the set to speed up the process.

I had a fight scene to do with Mr. Bronson. He was really good at stunt fighting. I wasn't bad at it myself. Two stuntmen had been flown down to double us in the dangerous parts of the fight. I was told he didn't like the looks of his double so they flew another stuntman down. It's a long way from L.A.

> **"In such beautiful surroundings there couldn't be any problems. Wrong! Most of them were called Charles."**

Came the day to shoot the fight and we were, cast and crew, ready. In the scene I'm smacking Camilla about her pretty face and Charles comes in and saves the day, and Camilla.

The prop men had built a chest of drawers and one of the drawers was a breakaway. The script called for Charles to grab that drawer, break it over my head, knocking me down on a bed. Then he lifts the bed with me on it and slams the two of us against the wall. Hanging on the wall is a thing, a decorative piece, made out of marlin spears. The spears points stick out in all directions like a sunburst. When Charles flattens me between the bed and the wall, the prop man was to pull a latch and the marlin spears fall and kill me.

I didn't want to do that part of the fight. There was nowhere for me to go to avoid those spears when that thing dropped and I'm a devout coward.

First, Charles wanted me to do the fight. He pointed to my double and said, "You don't want to look like that on the screen. Look at the gut on the guy."

Tony, my double started to turn purple. Not because he liked the color. It's called rage.

Tony had doubled Burt Lancaster his whole career. He's very good at what he does. He killed a man in a real fight and got off with manslaughter. Now the stunt coordinator has an immediate problem... how to get Tony far enough away that he doesn't kill our star. Last seen, Tony was headed for the airport.

Charles had another more pressing concern. He didn't want to hit me with the breakaway drawer. He picked up a twenty-gallon can. It was empty but it had eight metal corners. Now that it's been decreed that I would do my own fighting, I objected. Overruled.

Playing a Nazi officer, my costume was a long sleeved field jacket. It can hide elbow pads, arm pads, wristbands and hip pads. I put them all on. On the street, walking back to the set I pass the Mexican cameraman. He'd been a treat to work with - creative, fast and a great sense of humor. Out from under his hat comes a whisper, "Knock the head off the little S.O.B."

The prop men had rigged a wire on the marlin spear that pointed straight down. They would yank that wire to pull the point of the spear away from me when the plaque was released. Nervous? You bet your bippy!

"Action!" I start smacking Camilla; stunt smacks. They looked lethal but I missed her by a foot. Enter the hero. Charles swung the can back to hit me with it and yells, "Cut!" He really did mean cut. The metal handle had cut the palm side of three of his fingers.

He stood there, blood dripping, and the crew applauded. The nurse taped his fingers. The make-up man made up the tape and we did the whole stunt. Everything worked this time. The crew applauded again. I told you he was good.

Three weeks later we did the shot of the marlin spear going through my head. On my back with the camera close to the right side of my head, the prop men hid their special effects equipment on my left.

A flat metal bar went up my left side under my shirt curved around my shoulder up the left side of my neck, curved again around my cheek and across the front of my left eye. The whole thing was hidden from the camera by my body and nose. At the point where the metal passed my ear there was a spring mechanism that held the eight-inch point of a marlin spear.

The end of the bar, in front of my eye, had a hole in it. The prop man tied the bottom end of a very thin wire filament through that hole and handed the top end to another prop man standing ten feet above me on a ladder. He strung the wire through three two-foot long segments of marlin spear. The segments would telescope. When the first one was dropped down the wire and hit the bar protecting my eye, the second piece would slide down over the first, a split second later. The third segment would follow so fast it would look like one long piece had pierced my eye. In the half a second this happened, the catch on the spring behind my left ear would be released, and the tip of the spear would appear as if it had gone clear through my head.

I forgot to mention the rubber tube that went alongside the metal contraption. One end was attached to a pump. The open end was hidden from the camera behind the bridge of my nose - pressed between my eye and the end of the bar that was supposed to protect me from the falling segments of spear. When all the other action went on, another prop man was to pump make-up blood through the tube. It took several hours to get everything ready. I didn't sleep much.

Special care was taken with the lighting because I was pinned between the wall and the bed at this point in the fight - a definite challenge for the lighting crew.

Time to go. They rolled the camera and removed my head support making room for the spring action.

The camera operator was a giant. He had arms like legs. He was the only person I've ever met hairier than Robin Williams. On close-up shots he has the best view of the scene.

When the director yelled, "Cut" this giant walked over to me. I hadn't moved. I was covered with red liquid. He didn't say a word. He bent down, reached out his huge, hairy forearm and pointed at it. Every hair was standing on end.

> ## "The patient died. The movie was a bomb."

The location was perfect. The actors were more than competent. The director did a good job. The camera crew, the lighting guys and especially the prop department were exceptional. The wardrobe and make-up folks worked their tails off. It's not easy to make a person look like he lost an eye to a marlin.

The patient died. The movie was a bomb.

Charles was sitting in a folding chair on the only cobblestone street in the fishing village we shot in. A shy barefoot kid loafed by. I could tell he wanted to talk but didn't know how to start. Mr. Bronson hadn't been friendly to the natives.

Much to my surprise, he waved the kid over and motioned for him to sit down. He picked up a steel pipe and laid it across his lap. I couldn't hear them from where I was watching, but they seemed to understand each other. I'd guess the pipe was about four feet long and a one-quarter inch to three- eighths inch hole in it. Charles took a nail out of his pocket and then tore a strip of paper from a page in his script. He wrapped the paper around the head of the nail and inserted the nail, point first, in the end of the pipe.

Then they started pointing at a homemade wooden ladder on the flat roof of an adobe across the street. It was about thirty yards away. Charles held up two fingers. The kid shook his head "no" and held up three. Charles nodded in agreement, put the pipe up to his mouth and Whoosh! That nail went zinging and zapped into the third rung of the ladder.

That part of the script worked!

CHAPTER 18
THE NAME GAME

Wyleek Fantroy. I collect names of people. I know that most of the people in the world, if they heard it, would think my name sounds amusing. Well, for years I've made a list of names that amuse me. It's a game. It has rules. You can't use the phone book. You can collect names from books, newspaper articles, signs, billboards and from other people.

I've been playing the game so long that friends send me names. I've got a lot of names. Wyleek is one. Like Benny Hill said in one of his skits, "Just think of the imagination that Ephrem Zimbalist, Jr's. parents had when they named him."

Duke Shannon was the name of the scout I played on "Wagon Train." John Wayne was called Duke by most people... friends and fans. He was the top Western film star of his day. I don't know if that fact had anything to do with it, but the producers of "Wagon Train" wanted me to change my name to Duke Shannon.

I was twenty-four and kind of used to my name. It fit me. Dennis the Menace and Denny Dimwit were appropriate when I was a pain or a buffoon. I didn't want to change my name and I told them so.

They said that Denny didn't sound manly or mature. They said that first names ending in "Y" weren't right for leading men.

Hello. What about Jimmy Stewart, Henry Fonda, Tony Curtis, Harry Belafonte, Humphrey Bogart, Cary Grant and Sidney Poitier? The producers dropped that line of thought. But they didn't give up.

> **"I was twenty-four and kind of used to my name. It fit me... I didn't want to change my name and I told them so."**

Lots of people change their names. Some people change it to hide. Some people just don't like their given name. In Hollywood, the name change has to do with image and how the name will look in lights.

There was an agent who became notorious for changing actors' names. Henry Wilson came up with Rock Hudson, Tab Hunter, Tom Tryon, Ty Hardin and Cal Bolder. Times have changed. One of the biggest film stars in the world is Governor Arnold Schwarzenegger. That name seems to look just fine in lights, or as governor of a state.

There's nothing wrong with changing your name. In fact it can be the right move. Take Archibald Leach to Cary Grant. Or a change from Issur Danielovitch to Kirk Douglas and Leonard Sly to Roy Rogers and Francis Gumm to Judy Garland. Those changes turned out okay.

Tula Ellice Finklea changed her name to Lily Norwood then changed it to Cid and ended up Cyd Charisse. Some people get caught up in "the name game."

This is how we settled my name change. I said I wouldn't change my last name. My folks had named me in the first place so I said they would come up with a list of ten first names that they wouldn't object to. I'd give the list to the producers and they could pick from that list.

The producers picked Scott. I called my parents and told them. Dad said, "Great Scott," and Mom said "Scott Tissue." They always had a sense of humor.

So my billing on "Wagon Train" was Denny Miller at the start, Denny Scott Miller for a while, and finally, Scott Miller. As soon as my job on the Train ended I went back to Denny Miller.

> **"Like Shakespeare said, 'An actor by any other name would smell the same.'"**

Like Shakespeare said, "An actor by any other name would smell the same."

~~Denny~~ *Scott Miller.*

CHAPTER 19
PARADES

I love a parade. Many people do. So do the citizens of Ojai (pronounced Oh-Hi), California. It's a town of about 8,000 and most of them are in the Fourth of July parade. The ones who don't participate line the streets with chairs. People reserve a good seat by setting up their chairs along the curb, all along the parade route, on the main street (Ojai Avenue). Most people have reserved their spot two days early. By parade time you can't find a spot to squeeze in another chair. It's held on the Fourth of July so it's a happy affair. Red, white and blue everything. It's very festive.

There are sad parades too. The first parade I remember was in 1945, passing down Pennsylvania Avenue, passing the White House. Seated on Dad's shoulders, I could see everything. Most of the people around us were crying. You could hear them and see them.

When President Roosevelt's casket came in view there was a sad feeling in the air. Thinking back over the years, I don't remember ever having that feeling again. One other time when I was at bedside, when Dad died - then it was a feeling of sadness and being numb at the same time.

The next parade I saw, another Fourth of July, was also going down Pennsylvania Avenue, past the White House. The Montgomery Junior High School Band, dressed all in white except for shiny blue and gold capes, marched proudly by. My gold-colored coronet and I marched with them. We marched behind a horse platoon. Our white shoes were not white at the end of the parade. It's hard to watch where you step when you're reading music.

The Rose Bowl Parade is huge. It is very long with all the beautiful floats, equestrian groups, many bands and dignitaries. The Wagon Train cast was invited to be in the parade one year.

> "When President Roosevelt's casket came in view there was a sad feeling in the air. Thinking back over the years I don't remember ever having that feeling again."

Montgomery Hills Brass (aka Monkey Hills Jr. High).
Left to right: Billy Alford, the future Billy Kelso and Billy Cave.

We had to be there at five a.m. The participants were gathered down side streets just off the parade route. All the horse groups were assembled in a separate area. I didn't see why when I arrived. Shortly after we found our four parade horses, we were invited to a breakfast party being held in the huge home not sixty feet from our horses. It's part of the parade tradition. New Years Day—Party Time!

The wranglers would come and tell us when it came time to mount up and take our place in the parade. It was after nine a.m. when they did. We'd been having a four-hour breakfast. After we thanked our host and hostess, we headed for our mounts. We saw why the horses had been kept separate from the bands and flower floats. The steam rose slowly from the horses' contribution to this festive occasion. The four of us were relieved to ride on.

The Rose Bowl Parade is a "teeth-drying" experience. It takes hours to get to the end. There are thousands of people on both sides of the street to wave to and smile at. About half way through, your front teeth dry and your upper lip gets stuck to them. Funny feeling; the feeling of not being able to not smile. To get your lip down, you have to stick out your tongue and lick your teeth. When your mouth gets so dry the tongue doesn't work, you have to pull your lip gently off your teeth with your thumb and forefinger. Try that in front of thousands of people, not to mention the millions of TV viewers and not look silly. It can't be done.

At the end of the Rose Parade route there is a huge field where the horse trailers and wranglers are waiting. This is the only place along the parade they don't have crowd control.

Parade ready.

The people on both sides form a funnel getting so narrow that it's difficult to ride through.

Frank McGrath, the bearded Charlie Wooster on "Wagon Train," had one pet peeve. He hated to be mistaken for the actor who played the cook, Wishbone, on a rival TV Western series, "Rawhide."

A very noisy fan pushed people aside, waving his autograph book and yelling, "Wishbone – Wishbone, please sign my book!" Frank wheeled his horse on the poor fellow and the last sight we had of the two, Frank's horse was right on the heels of the guy with Frank bellowing, "I'll Wishbone you!" I'm sure Wishbone lost a fan that day.

Frank had bad luck in the Thanksgiving Day Parade in Chicago. We were to be on horseback again. Frank asked if all the horses were trained for parade riding. "Oh yes," replied the wrangler. Frank's horse jumped every crosswalk in the parade. The spectators were fortunate that Frank was an outstanding horseman. If it had been my horse, I'd have been bucked off in the first block and the horse would be on his own, probably creating problems among the people lining the street. Frank and his horse were very tired at the end of that parade.

Virginia City, Nevada is not a city. It's a small town with a large history. The richest strike in the West of silver and gold was made right under its streets.

In May, 1964, the Business Men's Club of Virginia City invited the cast of Wagon Train to be in their parade.

At a dinner the night before the parade, we were each given a belt buckle by the club. I have never seen a finer buckle. Carved on the front is a figure of an 1849 miner and his provision-loaded burro. The buckle is three-inches high and four-inches wide. It is solid gold. Mounted in the middle is a $20 U.S. gold coin, dated 1907. They gave one to all six of us. There must be a few secret veins of gold left under the town.

The next morning the parade lasted about ten minutes. The route was six blocks long. We felt so guilty wearing our new gold buckles that we turned the parade around and headed back through town.

No one was there. The folks had gone into the casinos and saloons that lined Main Street, to continue their gambling and carousing. We stopped the parade and shot our guns in the air to let them know we were back. A few people came to the swinging doors to see what the noise was about.

"We've seen you guys already, c'mon and join the party!" they yelled. So we tied up our horses and joined them. That's the only parade I know of that never ended.

I recently moved to Las Vegas, Nevada. Virginia City is a short drive north. I'm going up there soon wearing my gold buckle and thank the Men's Club again. I wonder if part of the parade is still parked in the middle of town. It's only been forty years.

CHAPTER 20
THE WIZARD OF AHS

Dennis Shives lives in his Volkswagen bus. On the tiny shelf under the windshield sits an abondoned hummingbirds' nest. A thousand-year-old, hand-shaped flint spear-point sits next to the nest. A dried flower, a shark's tooth, some moss, a cactus skeleton and seashells, a smooth river rock and a small brilliantly-colored "something" make up the rest of his traveling companions.

His shirts and pants hang from a wire stretched across one windowless side of the bus just above his mattress. Open the back door and there on a shelf over the engine is a large box full of tools. Drills, hammers, pliers, screwdrivers, chisels; all he needs to build or fix anything. I mean anything, from a parade float that actually floats to a beautiful house on stilts in Alaska.

Dennis Shives.

Another box contains tools you've never seen before. At least I'd never seen before. These he uses to create sand sculptures. There are large wooden rollers for putting the finishing touches on his work... scales for a fish, hair for a bear, buff for a Model T. He made all these tools. Take these trowels, scoops, small shovels, tampers; some tools with no name along with the rollers and add a sandy beach and Dennis will create magic. Kids of all ages gather round and stay for hours.

How good is he at building anything out of sand? When he shows up at the beach, any beach on the west coast from Canada to Mexico, the other contestants know they're competing for second place.

Wooden carvings can be found almost everywhere in the bus. There's a baby's spoon

Dennis Shives creates a charging rhino.

with an airplane handle for "zoom, zoom" feeding, a door knocker in the shape of a womans breast; ten or twelve Harry Potter wands made out of exotic woods; a few x-rated carvings and maybe an unfinished unicorn or two.

Dennis paints beautifully in oils and watercolors and does intricate pen and ink drawings. He sculpts in stone, clay, wood, a compound much like cement, gold, silver and jade.

He invents things, fun things made from whimsy, wit and wonder. They are toys for kids of all ages. A wind-powered bubble machine and a breath bubble blower that reloads itself with soapy water.

He invented a toy he calls a "meadow dancer." It's very light and can be held in your hand. It plays music as you walk, skip or jog along. It's driven by wind.

You see when Dennis holds a tool in his hands, whether it's a paint brush, a sand roller or a screwdriver, it becomes a part of him. He can't tell where his hand ends and the tool begins.

He sculpted a four-foot wide, seven-foot tall charging rhino for me. He even put a Mastercard in its' mouth. He also carved a wooden dragon and a life-sized lion's head out of a piece of rare burl wood, for me. The lion is gray and gold and looks like Bert Lahr in the "Wizard of Oz."

He is the kindest, happiest, most talented and creative man I know. I think he gets his energy from the wind. The same wind that powers his toys. If there is a freer spirit, and I doubt there is, I'd sure like to meet it. I am privileged to be one of his friends.

Oh, I forgot to tell you — he plays a mean harmonica.

A very special Golden Lion.

Mountain Dreamer.

CHAPTER 21
STAYING ALIVE

There was a time when some actors looked down on television and film. Some still do. To them, the only worthwhile acting jobs were on live stage with the Broadway stage being the ultimate place to act.

To do a TV commercial was a sin; if not a sin, then certainly beneath these actors. They wouldn't be seen using their talent to sell a product. Then Joseph Cotton did a TV spot for Bayer Aspirin. Bette Davis sold another product. And they made a bundle of money doing it. Many more big stars followed.

Hello! Maybe it's not tainted work. Maybe I can make enough money in commercials to be selective in my other acting offers. I can turn down the part of the third heavy that only has three lines and wait for a better part. Today big name stars like Sean Connery, James Garner, Sam Elliott and Demi Moore even do voice-overs for TV commercials and animated characters.

The TV series "Wagon Train" did more to break down the cast system than any other show. A juicy part was offered to a film star each week. The episode would be named after the character they would play and they would be paid handsomely. It worked for the actors and it made the show #1 in the ratings.

> **"To do a TV commercial was a sin; if not a sin, then certainly beneath these actors."**

I was a misplaced basketball player and was elated when I was hired to do the part of Duke Shannon (assistant scout to Robert Horton) on "Wagon Train." I didn't know at the time it would be a job that lasted over three years and one hundred seven episodes. Later, I did twenty-six episodes of a sit-com "Mona McClusky," starring Juliet Prowse. I enjoyed the feeling you get when you have a steady job. For me, it was a relaxing feeling and besides, I enjoyed the work and especially the people I worked with.

During my first year on "the train," my part was so small that when a cow-poke would ride up to me and ask, "Which way did they go?" I'd just shrug. The character I played didn't know. The second year, when the same question was asked, I got to point and say, "That-a-away!" The third year Duke Shannon was a more trusted scout and sometimes, when asked "Which way?" he replied, "Follow me!" Those three years were the best acting school an actor could possibly attend. I got to watch and work with almost every big-name star in Hollywood.

That was many years ago. It was so much fun having a recurring role that each time I've been hired to do a guest role on a TV series since, I go through a routine.

The minute I get the script I leaf through it and find the first line the character I'm to play has to say. I tab the top of that page and continue to search out every line and every other appearance the character has in the story. I already know the part is of a good guy or a heavy.

I'm looking to see if the character gets killed or sent to jail or disappears. Why? I want to know if this could be a recurring role, one of the running cast. I really like working. My dream jobs have been in a show's regular cast, being part of a team, a family.

In over forty-five years it has only happened four times. First, on "Wagon Train" and then on "Mona McClusky." I did four episodes of "Dallas." The other time I played the sheriff on the Canadian version of "Lonesome Dove."

Canada was a joy, the Canadians a bigger joy! My character got killed in the third episode. I didn't feel too good either. To be honest, I was broken-hearted.

"Northwest Passage," starring Buddy Ebsen and Keith Larson, was an MGM frontier series. I got a role in it and the minute I got the script, I went through my search routine.

The character spoke first and on page three. That was a very good sign. On the twentieth page he got shot. Not good. On the twenty-first page, he fell into a lake and didn't surface. Still I continued my search. Maybe one of his buddies would pull him out, and he would live to work again. On the twenty-second page, a cannon was fired causing an avalanche, which filled the lake.

In two pages my character was killed twice and buried. Undaunted, I asked the director if they planed any flashbacks that involved my character. "Not a chance," he answered.

Sunday

THE INDIANAPOLIS STAR
Magazine
January 5, 1964

Scott Miller . . . A Hoosier Rides West With Wagon Train (Story Inside)

Riding "the train" and having a ball!

CHAPTER 22
APPLES AND ORANGES

Not long ago Arnold Palmer was voted "Athlete of the Century." Some magazine sponsored the contest. I'm not sure which one.

I don't know Mr. Palmer. I've heard he is a nice guy. I know he is a great golfer. I watched him play in his prime. Not many golfers could beat him. Nicklaus, Watson and a few others beat him every once in a while, but not very often.

Arnold Palmer was one of the greatest golfers, ever. "Athlete of The Century?" Granted you have to have an agile mind to excel in golf. To stand the mental pressures in tournament competition, agility of the mind can and does make the difference between winning and losing. But an agile body is not a prerequisite.

Strength to hit the ball farther than your opponent is an advantage. And you have to have endurance to walk the course. This does not include carrying your clubs and bag. This does not include running even one yard.

Jonathan Winters has a routine that goes: "If you play golf, you have to have lots of special clubs and a bag to hold them. You have to have golf balls, a golf glove, golf shoes, golf tees and a towel to wipe the dirt off your clubs. You have to go to a golf course and pay a fee to play, and a fee to rent an electric cart, and if you're a serious golfer, a fee for a caddie to tell you how the greens play."

Golf courses are built in the most beautiful places in the world. They are located amongst magnificent mountains; rivers and streams run through them, oceans border them, and lovely forests grow by the fairways. In every direction there is overwhelming beauty.

The golfer takes all his stuff and pays all his fees and goes out on a bright, sunny day and looks at his feet for five hours.

Now compare the average golfer with the average football player, or basketball player, or ping-pong player, gymnast, fencer or badminton player. The only thing the golfer will excel at is his age. He can play golf to a ripe old age. They even have a Senior Professional Golfers' Association.

The point is, when you are handing out "Best Athlete Awards," be more sport specific, more event-specific... "Best 100 Meter Backstroke Swimmer"; "Best Archer"; "Best Golfer Under Fifty."

"Best Athlete of The Century" sells magazines, I guess.

The profession of acting has its own obsession with "Best." "Best Actor of 2003" makes as much sense as "Best Athlete of The Century." None!

The Oscars, (the Academy Awards) are silly. If there were a contest between five actors playing Hamlet it would make more sense, but still would be a popularity contest.

Until recently, comedy films were lumped in with dramatic films. The only films not included in "Best Actor Award" are documentaries and animated films. It's apples and oranges.

In our society dramatic actors are almost always given "The Best" awards over their brother actors performing in comedic roles. For some reason if, as an actor, you can make people cry, get angry or depressed, you are more talented than an actor who has the talent to make people laugh.

Comedy is not serious. Never could figure that one out. A writer or an actor can say the most serious thing in a book, in a script, or in a play, on stage, or in film wrapped in comedy. A little bit of sugar helps the medicine go down.

The Oscars sell tickets. The winning film gets a boost at the box office. Wouldn't more films make more money if the five nominees in each category were awarded Oscars? All five actors and actresses would have the validation of their fellow professionals. All five films the actors played in would make more money and the Oscars would have meaning.

This is not solely my idea. Some actors have refused the Oscar for these same reasons. In1971, George C. Scott didn't accept his Oscar for his work in "Patton."

"Best Five Performances in a Comedy by an Actor," "Best Five Performances by an Actress in a Drama," "Best Golfer of the Century." It's a Win-Win situation!

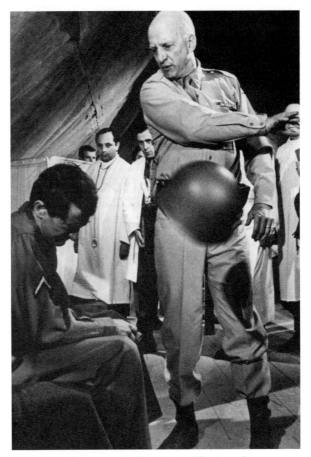

George C. Scott as "Patton."

Martin Smiddy — A real FANatic!

CHAPTER 23
PAPER FANS

Paper friends. I have a few. One day a letter arrives from a perfect stranger and years later I find a perfect friend.

Winifred Franks wrote and told my mother (Mom was answering my fan mail at the time) that she enjoyed watching "Wagon Train" in her flat outside of London. She wrote again and again, always on sky blue paper. Her Cockney way of saying things reminded me of Eliza Doolittle in "My Fair Lady." (George Cukor received a best director Oscar for the 1964 film starring Audrey Hepburn and Rex Harrison).

Winnie's letters were friendly, but feisty. You could tell she wanted to be a friend, not a bother. She came on the wings of laughter and never, never landed on the septic tank of life. She was a genuine, jolly person and it wasn't long after I read one of her letters that I wrote back.

We had this paper conversation for many years. During that time, she knitted sixteen sweaters for me, gave my mother an antique glove ring, gave me a collection of ornate antique keys and many other lovely gifts.

Her "Budgie" (pet bird) died and I sent her a little money to buy another. I phoned her on several holidays and she sounded like she wrote, like Eliza.

My parents arranged to meet her on their way round the world, on one of Dad's sabbaticals. She didn't show up. No explanation was offered. Soon after, her letters stopped; again, no explanation.

Several years later, she started writing

> **"She was a genuine, jolly person and it wasn't long after I read one of her letters that I wrote back."**

again. She had found a long lost aunt that was ill and needed help. Winnie cared for her until she passed away. She wrote that she was well and we enjoyed her presence in our lives again. Her letters were written by three people. The first part was always by Winnie. Sometimes one page, other times four or five. Then she would send her best regards and sign Winnie.

At the bottom of the page, the other two "people", a boy and a girl, would add their thoughts. They were drawn in stick figures under her name. These imaginary people could be more intimate. They could send their love and say they missed me, things like that.

It was like Edgar Bergen's Charlie McCarthy. These people, Flo and Fred, were Winnie's alter ego. Webster defines it as a second self, an intimate friend, a constant companion. Winnie's second self could talk through these stick figures. I've never had letters like them; letters from three people written by one. I still have them.

Winnie and I never met. We were always at least six thousand miles apart. I never saw a photo of her. I heard her voice several times. And yet she is a dear friend. I hope she is well.

Martin Smiddy is another paper friend. We have been writing for twenty years. I've been to visit him and his family in Wales, and he dropped by my place in California, twice.

He's a physical educator as is his wife, Kate. He is also a Tarzan fan. He has a collection of Edgar Rice Burroughs memorabilia that grows each month, with each payday. Winnie and he are my best distant friends along with George McWhorter.

George is the curator of rare books at the University of Louisville Library. He cares for the largest Edgar Rice Burroughs collection in the world.

Tarzan fans gather each year to buy and sell books, lobby posters, 8x10s, toys, buttons, buckles etc. These gatherings are called "Dum-Dums" - the sound of the drums bringing the natives together. Fans attend from all over the world. A first edition Tarzan book, in good condition, can bring $10,000. These are serious collectors. George has hosted four of these yearly get-togethers. There's one coming up soon, and I'll be there.

George will start the meeting with a Tarzan yell. He was an opera singer in his youth. No one sleeps when he yells. He can break glass.

George is another reason for me to be thankful that I played Tarzan forty-five years ago. His letters are full of humor. He is the editor of the Burroughs Bulletin. It is, without question, the highest quality fanzine in existence. He is also the editor of this book; another reason for me to be grateful. If these pages have any merit, it will be due to George McWhorter's touch.

> "He was an opera singer in his youth. No one sleeps when he yells. He can break glass."

Not all fan mail is as rewarding as the mail from these good friends. I received a letter from Africa years ago. It went something like this: "Please not to send any more of your photos to Bwana Ngoro Nogoro, for I am finding them in his toilet." The name has been changed to protect the guilty.

I now have a website: www.denny-miller.com The dash is necessary because another Denny Miller beat me to it. I still have a few requests for photos. Most of them come from the Scandinavian countries; probably because I'm the only Nordic type to play the role of Tarzan besides Buster Crabbe.

All my 8x10's come with a guarantee:

My pictures seem to scare the little creatures to death.

CHAPTER 24
FRIEND

"Sorry."

"No talking during the meeting unless you have the floor," the president replied.

"I was just telling a joke. Want to hear it?"

"No! You're fined five dollars!"

"Make that ten dollars," the pres roared.

What a difference two years makes. I had been among thousands of GI's occupying Germany in 1956 and 1957. It was a good duty. No one was shooting at us. The food was great. I had been honorably discharged and was back at UCLA.

Part of campus life was fraternity meetings. This was the first one I had attended for over two years. At the last one I had sat on the back row with my best friend, Don Allison, and told jokes. At this meeting I was still on the back row, but Don was up front. He was the pres now.

He doesn't know this, but I saved our friendship back then. I paid the fine. I had lots of money. The GI Bill paid one hundred ten dollars a month. But I didn't go to any more meetings till Don graduated that spring. We've been best friends for over half a century. I was a jock, played basketball, so I was excused from meetings anyway. Besides I could never remember the secret knock and handshake.

> ## "I still prefer women with arms even if they have wings as well."

Don and I and eighty other students went on a tour of Europe in the summer of '54. In two months, we saw every museum in fourteen countries. We even went to Yugoslavia. It was a beautiful country back then. Professor George Kneller led the tour. For twenty-four summers, he taught class in busses and trains and boats all through Europe.

Over two thousand students had a more vivid picture of Europe and its' history thanks to the professor. They also carried a bundle of beautiful memories for the rest of their lives.

I remember leading the stream of kids into the Louvre in Paris. Just inside the entrance we were greeted by a magnificent marble statue. I turned and ran back through the crowd yelling, "It's even more beautiful than I thought. The Venus de Milo is spectacular!"

The professor whispered in my ear, "That's Winged Victory." I kept quiet during the rest of the tour through the museum. Venus de Milo turned out to be very beautiful, but Winged Victory... well even with the wrong name, she was spectacular.

What a trip. We got to jitterbug on the lawn where St. Francis of Assisi used to walk. We bought fireworks in Liechtenstein and a few stamps with the little money left over. We sang a few songs in the Red Ox Gasthaus with some students from Heidelberg U. We saw the midnight sun from a hill in Bergen, Norway. We sailed through the edge of a hurricane on a student ship of the Holland American line. When the storm hit, 300 students disappeared from the ship's dining room in nine minutes. We floated down the Stavanger Fjord surrounded by tall blond people with oriental-shaped, cobalt blue eyes.

Don Allison, my life-time best friend.
A serious scamp!

I had so much fun that I joined the tour the next two summers. When the professor and kids would come by the Army base in Germany where I was stationed, I'd hitch a ride. One summer they took me to Switzerland. The next summer I joined them in Denmark and got to see the sun go in a circle again.

Forty years later I was lucky to be cast to do a TV commercial in Paris. I was sure not to mix up the two ladies in marble. Venus and Ms. Victory were just as beautiful as I remembered. I still prefer women with arms even if they have wings as well.

Don and I have shared our lives. Lasting friendships get better even if our memories don't. He and his wife, Janet, just attended my daughter Cortney's wedding. I hope Cortney and Bill, fifty years from now, can look back on their lives and say, "We've had a good friend all our lives, just like Dad and Don!"

CHAPTER 25
POITIER AND BELAFONTE

Durango, Mexico is in a high desert. This means it's dry, very dry. That means it's dusty. In the spring the dust devils can knock you off your feet, fill your eyes and mouth with grit, make eating outside impossible, and spook your horse. I've never seen a discount travel deal to Durango.

All that means it's a perfect place to shoot Western films. That's why I was there for three months. I was going to work with Harry Belafonte and Sidney Poitier in, "Buck and the Preacher." I'll eat sand any day for that opportunity. It was Poitier's debut as a director and he also played the part of Buck. You guessed it – Harry was the Preacher.

Cameron Mitchell was the main heavy and I played his nephew, a stupid bundle of angry nerves. One of Jeff Foxworthy's definitions describes the role I played. "If you whistle through your tooth—you just might be a redneck."

My character's goal was to get Buck's wagon train of slaves to turn back to the plantations. Having been declared free, the goal of the folks on the black wagon train was to settle farmland out west and to start a new life as free people.

I had done one hundred ten episodes of the TV series "Wagon Train." You would expect me to be a handy horseman. You would be wrong. Even with all those hours on a horse, people could still read a newspaper between my butt and the saddle. When it came to horsemanship, I was still a basketball player, bouncing all over the place.

The first shot in "Buck and the Preacher" was a long shot of the bad guys riding into town. About fifteen of us gathered about half a mile away from the camera. Sidney yelled, "Come on!" and we were off. Cameron had the fastest horse and it was a race to him. The rest of the guys

COLUMBIA PICTURES
Presents

SIDNEY POITIER · HARRY BELAFONTE

Before they can settle the West, they have to settle their score.

BUCK and The PREACHER

RUBY DEE · CAMERON MITCHELL

Screenplay by ERNEST KINOY · Story by ERNEST KINOY and DRAKE WALKER · Music by BENNY CARTER
Produced by JOEL GLICKMAN · Directed by SIDNEY POITIER   An E & R /BEI PRODUCTION
COLOR   (M)

Harry Belefonte was terrific as "The Preacher."

were stunt men, real cowboys. Among them my double, Walter Scott, made a good living riding broncs on the rodeo circuit.

And then there was me. I was in last place before we started. When Cameron got to the camera, I was fifty yards back. Everybody was there when I rode up demonstrating one of my patented stops.

When I finally got my nag to stop, my right foot was hooked around the pommel, my right arm circled the horse's neck behind his ears, the horse's nose was in my left armpit and I was looking down the horse's left ear. Sydney pretended not to notice and suggested we do it again, at a little slower pace.

Cameron didn't take direction sometimes and it took three takes and some prodding from two of the stunt men for the group to arrive as a group. After that for twelve weeks, Walter Scott, my double, rode all over that high desert and made me look great.

The best directors I've worked with, Sydney Pollock, George Cukor, Vincente Minelli, Virgil Vogel, Sidney Poitier and many others create a calm relaxed atmosphere on the set. Everyone, especially the actors, can have the courage to go for it... "It" being to let their characters come to life in the telling of the story they're working in. They can go out on a limb and know that the director will catch them if they fall, or if they go too far or not far enough.

On top of a windy bleak mountain, we were rehearsing a scene between the sheriff and I. A very good Mexican character actor played the sheriff. There was an argument that ends up with me cutting the sheriff's throat. After we did it three times, Sidney

> **"Actors who play heavies die a lot. They hit the ground, bite the dirt and the hero walks off with the pretty gal and his friends tag along singing a song."**

motioned for me to follow him and walked off a distance from the cast and crew. I followed.

He turned to me and took one step so our eyes were less than a foot apart. Not taking his eyes from mine he whispered, "I just don't believe you hate us niggers enough." He smiled and walked back to the set.

There it was. In his first job as a director, he knew, as the director, he was a safety net. He was saying, you could go bananas in this scene, go as far as you want and I'll catch you if you go too far. It didn't surprise me. After all he had won an Oscar for Best Actor.

We rehearsed the scene again and I added a large dose of hate. When we finished, I looked at Sidney. His nod made me feel so good I almost burst.

Actors who play heavies die a lot. They hit the ground, bite the dirt and the hero walks off with the pretty gal and his friends tag along singing a song.

My character dies in this film in a way that leaves no doubt that if the film is made into a TV series, he won't be in it.

Harry Belafonte's role as a preacher is like no other preacher on film. Ever!

You can't call this preacher's Bible "The good book." It's really a holster. It's a handy place to hide a double-barreled, sawed-off shotgun. When Harry's preacher takes up a collection, he really TAKES a collection.

When I peek over a rock to get a good shot at Harry, he blasts me with that shotgun. Keep in mind... as I've said before, I'm a devout coward. Not the character I'm playing. Me!

The Mexican special-effects crew showed me their special air-compressed blowgun. They let me watch them load its inch-wide barrel with a Max Factor blood containing hundreds of little pieces of sponge in it. It's a close-shot. I peek over the rock and WHOOSH goes their air gun and my face is instant raw hamburger. Ugly? Very!

There's an instant hustle and bustle of hands with towels, hands with a folding chair to sit in. Inquiring minds want to know if I'm all right. More hands with what seems to be a gallon of Murine... Lots of blinking... I'm okay. Okay until I hear the camera operator tell Sidney that I blinked too soon. We'll have to do it again.

"The show must go on." I'll kill whoever came up with that slogan. Of course, we did it again. This time it worked but it took two gallons of Murine. I looked like I'd cried my eyes out for two days. But I lived to die another day, two or three times, if I'm lucky.

"Buck and the Preacher" is a good western movie. Rent it and take a look.

CHAPTER 26
CALL ME CHICKEN

Chicken. You've heard that rattlesnake tastes like chicken. I'll never find out for sure. I'm content to eat chicken. I like it most ways it can be cooked. But I'm chicken to eat rattlesnake.

"Lijah" was one of the best parts I ever got to play. "Lijah" was the title of an episode on "Gunsmoke." The script was written by Bill Blinn, who also created, "The Rookies" and "Eight Is Enough."

The character, Lijah, was a mountain man. He didn't get along with folks because of an unhappy childhood, so he became a loner. He was a trapper and dressed in animal skins. In fact, from a distance, he looked like a moving hill of animals. A tail here, buckskin there, a

Lijah.

large quilted coat, pants, boots and shirt made of skins. The only store-bought thing he wore was his hat. He had two weather beaten felt hats. Why two? One hat leaked on the side and one hat leaked on top. So he sewed one hat inside the other. That solved the leak problem. He was a practical man.

He was also deaf. My mother is deaf. It can be a lonely, frightening life being deaf. But playing the part of a deaf person presents unique challenges for a hearing actor. You can't react to the other actors when they speak to you. You can't react to other noises like... the rattle of a snake.

In the script, Lijah goes down in an old well to save a little girl he saw fall in. This little girl was played by Erin Moran. Lijah called her "Lady Bug". You may remember her from the many years she starred in "Happy Days."

In the walls of the old well are some niches. These niches are home to two rattlesnakes.

The set designers built a twenty-five foot high tube on the sound stage. The inside of the tube looked just like an old well. There was scaffolding and steps alongside so the actors and the camera crew could get to the top.

The well was built in sections to allow one section to be removed so the camera could be placed at the bottom to shoot up through the well. A canvas painting of sky was stretched above the open mouth of the well.

They were going to use real, live rattlesnakes in the niches. The snake wrangler let me watch him stitch the snakes' mouths shut. One stitch on each front side so the

> "The wrangler explained that it did no good to pull the fangs out because there were little baby fangs under the big ones. In other words the snake could gum you to death. I watched the stitching with undivided attention."

snake could stick his tongue out but couldn't open its mouth. The wrangler explained that it did no good to pull the fangs out because there were little baby fangs under the big ones. In other words the snake could gum you to death. I watched the stitching with undivided attention.

The camera was ready at the bottom, shooting up through the space of well that had been removed. I was at the top ready to skooch down the well. My back was against the wall and my feet were in front of me on the opposite wall. The idea was to inch my way down buttocks first.

The wrangler put the two rattlers in their niches and I waited for the director's call,

"Action!" It didn't come. Instead I heard feet scrambling and cursing below me.

The rattlers had fallen out of their niches. I climbed up and out onto the scaffold. Chaos. While the snake wrangler kept repeating, "It's okay –It's okay!" The human pinball machine; people bouncing off each other trying to get away told me it's NOT OKAY as far as they were concerned!

The snakes were corralled and calm restored. The director said, "Before we all take our places, try placing the snakes again." On the second attempt, third and fourth, the results were the same. The snakes spilled out onto the floor.

The snakes were too big or the niches too small. Either way, the shot would be postponed till tomorrow while smaller rattlers were found. For me, that was like having a dental appointment called off for a day. I didn't get much sleep that night.

Like I have said before, I have been a devout coward most of my life. I remember when I first saw "The Thing." James Arness was absolutely frightening as the monster. It was no help that he was described in the film as a giant carrot. I got no sleep that night either. I've hated carrots ever since.

The new rattlers were much smaller and fit in their niches. The camera was ready. I was in my awkward seated position at the top of the well. I would inch my way down, down past the snakes to save Erin, who didn't have to be there in this shot.

"Action!" Down I went. I reached out for support. My arm went right in front of the rattlers. It's dark inside the well and remember, Lijah can't hear their warning rattles. I react as if one of the snakes hits me in the arm like the script calls for and continue to the bottom of the well. The snakes were still in place, asleep for all I know. I'm just thankful that neither one tried to bite me. "Cut" yells the director.

You can always tell if something hasn't gone right in a shot. The director gets together with the camera operator for a little conference. Kinda quiet, so no one can hear them. They were having one of those talks.

The director walked over to me and asked, "Do you think you could do it again?"

"I guess so." I mumbled. "What went wrong?"

He whispered, "Your eyes were so bugged out, nobody would believe you didn't know those rattlers were there."

I told you I was chicken when it comes to rattlesnakes.

CHAPTER 27
LIGHTS OUT

Two guys were holding me up. Another stunt man was holding my head trying to stop it from wobbling around like I didn't have control of it, which I didn't. My upper lip was throbbing and wasn't acting like my upper lip, and both knees were wobbling so much that one second I was six-foot four-inches tall, and the next I was five-foot four-inches tall. Thank goodness the guys holding my arms would catch me on the way to five-foot four.

"Are ya' okay? ARE YA' OKAY?" someone asked. "How should I know?" I flobbered. "I just got here." My upper lip worked like a board when I talked.

I over-corrected, my head bounced forward, and I got a quick glance at my feet. Someone had been bleeding on my shoes. That was a good thing, I thought. At least I could focus.

I heard some distant voice call, "I think he's gonna need stitches. Get a car over here." In my fuzzy brain that message translated, "Oh good, a car is going to stitch him up."

Someone else suggested that I sit down, an idea I agreed with. So I did. The two guys at my sides had to save me once more and guided me to an apple box.

See, when you are an actor and like doing your own stunt fights... I had slipped on some gravel and my face was just eleven inches left and ten inches in front of where it should have been. Tim Rosivitch, a two hundred forty-six pound, six-foot six-inch, ex-line backer for the Pittsburgh Steelers, just

> **"Tim Rosivitch, a two hundred forty-six pound, six-foot six-inch, ex-line backer for the Pittsburgh Steelers, just did what we had rehearsed. He threw a right cross. My teeth have never been the same."**

did what we had rehearsed. He threw a right cross. My teeth have never been the same. I was the one that goofed.

Stunt fights are like a dance. They are rehearsed by schooled stuntmen and women. Done right they look very realistic and no one gets hurt. They're planned, choreographed and done over and over in slow motion. Punches missed landing by at least a foot. When the person receiving the punch snaps his head in the direction the punch is thrown just as it goes by his head, you'd swear the punch landed. The hand and the head are quicker than the eye. Stuntman Yakima Canutt and John Wayne created this method of movie screen fighting. Before their genius, screen fights looked like a bunch of sissies pushing and shoving and playing patty-cake, patty-cake.

I went off to the nearest hospital, had the gash on the inside of my upper lip stitched up and went back to the set. Then we did the fight scene again. This time, with stitches in my lip and cotton up my nose and taking care not to slip in the gravel, the fight went like it should have the first time around.

The next day, for the only time in forty-five years, I wore a ski mask. It was a robbery scene. By this time my lip preceded my nose by an inch. I looked like Bart Simpson. I looked a lot like Bart Simpson! The mask covered up the lip problem. The only other scene I had to do was in a bar. I hid my lip behind a full, foaming beer mug. That shows why stunt people are important. An actor gets hurt doing his own stunt fighting and the production is in trouble.

Several months later and fourteen hours in a dental chair, a bone graft taken from my right jaw and transplanted to the upper left to shore up those loose teeth and I was like new. Universal Studios picked up the bill. I heard it came to over $25,000! Thank you very much.

> **"Seeing stars in Hollywood is usually fun, but not when they appear after a punch in the mouth."**

All of this happened on a show called "When The Whistle Blows". When I came back to the set after being sewn up, I found Tim off by himself crying. He was a pro and blamed himself. I told him it was old klutzy me and we had a good laugh about it. I sure was glad I was his friend. Seeing stars in Hollywood is usually fun, but not when they appear after a punch in the mouth.

One other thing: the morning after the accident, I was home getting dressed to go to work and I noticed a red welt running across my chest. My lip and teeth had all of my attention and the welt never made it to my pain center.

I asked a few questions at work about my mystery welt. Seems when Tim cold-cocked me I flew back and landed on my back, out like a veggie. Then the only stuntwoman in the group of eight stunt folks blasted me with a breakaway two by four across my front side. In rehearsals I had always been on my hands and knees at that point in the fight. Then the welt would have been in the right place, on my back. You ever had one of those days?

CHAPTER 28
ACTING WITH THE LORD

"Hawaii Five–0" was Jack Lord. James MacArthur was his sidekick, but Jack Lord was "the Man." I had heard rumors that Jack was difficult to work with. Not so.

I've only had three parts offered me that called for me to cry. I've managed to keep the child in me alive. That may be the reason that crying hasn't been a problem for me as an actor. More likely, the writer has written a scene that is so emotional that it is hard not to cry. That certainly was the case when I played the character on Five–0.

This character was accused of killing his fiancée. That was sad enough to make a strong man cry. Add to this the fact that the character had been so drunk at the time of her murder that he couldn't remember whether or not he'd killed her. I cried when I first read the script.

I was being interrogated by Jack Lord, in the crying scene. We had gotten off to a good start when someone dropped a hammer off screen. Jack jumped up and chased the guy off the sound stage into the street. When he came back, he still hadn't calmed down. He went to his mark, seated on his desk, and just sat there. When he was in control he made a short speech. No, he made a command. He said, "Give this man some consideration. This is a very difficult scene and I want complete silence!" I thanked him for his kindness,

The attitude of the cast and crew takes on the personality of the star of the show in a TV series. If the star cares, they care. The work is a joy, but the hours are long and a leader is needed. The star is that leader.

> "We had gotten off to a good start when someone dropped a hammer off screen. Jack jumped up and chased the guy off the sound stage into the street."

Jack's professional attitude made that scene one of the best I've done in 45 years.

The next night we shot my "drunk scenes". The camera truck was attached to a low flat bed trailer. The motorcycle I was to ride was cabled to the trailer. Most camera trucks are small trucks. When its bed is loaded with the camera, the camera operator, the cameraman, the lighting crew, the lights, the sound man and the director and the assistant director, it looks like one of those bicycle acts in the circus with all fifteen members of a family hanging on.

The truck was loaded. The character I'm playing is loaded and we're off. It's a Saturday night and we're going down the main street, Ala Moana, in Honolulu. We were in bumper-to-bumper traffic.

The director yelled his directions over the traffic noise. "Swerve back and forth as much as you can. Put your feet up on the handlebars. Stand up. Sit side saddle!" All the moves a drunken rider would do. I was having fun.

We stopped at a red light and out of the corner of my eye I see five real bikers pull to a stop. I gave them a half-hearted wave and they in turn gave me a look that translated to, "You dweeb. You're an absolute dork!"

When the light changed, just to prove them wrong, I grabbed the handle- bars, scrunched down like I was going 100 miles an hour and yelled… "VROOM-VROOM!!!!!!"

Jack was in charge.

CHAPTER 29
TARZAN X-RATED?

I DON'T THINK SO.

Los Angeles means the City of Angels. Who else but a city of angels would ban all Tarzan books from its public libraries because some librarian claimed the books were X-rated. Why? Tarzan and Jane were living in sin. They weren't married. Or so this librarian said.

On page 314 of "The Return of Tarzan," Jane and Tarzan tie the knot. Yep. It's right there on page 314. Would a librarian ban a series of books he or she hadn't read? This one did. To quote James Thurber in his book "*The 13 Clocks*," "If you have nothing better to do, you are somewhat less than much, and only a little more than anything." I bet this librarian was so colorful that he or she could disappear in a crowd of two.

During this ban, Edgar Rice Burroughs received a request from a Mrs. A. Nicely for a set of books for the Tarzana Library. E.R.B. replied that since the main library had barred his works, he could not grant a request from one of its branches.

He also wrote, *"I also feel that books that the Los Angeles Public Library believe might contaminate the morals or literary tastes of their readers should not be tolerated in Tarzana, and when we consider that some hundred million readers all over the world have already been contaminated, we should exert every effort to keep Los Angeles the one bright spot in the literary firmament."*

I know I would have liked Edgar a lot.

I have recently moved from the angelic region of California to "Sin City" – Las Vegas. A city, like most everything, is what you make of it. If you live on the east coast of the U.S., the west coast, especially the City of Angeles, is a wasteland. More books are sold in the Los Angeles area than any other place in the world. Wasteland? What's wrong with this picture?

Sin City? Las Vegas has more acreage devoted to outdoor recreational parks than any city of comparable size. But they also have more show girls and topless shows and more show girls and... Just in case, I wanted to be politically correct so my Nevada license plate reads:

"XTARZAN"

Do you think my car would be banned in Los Angeles?

CHAPTER 30
FOR CRYING OUT LOUD

Around the world there are four fictional characters known to almost everyone - Batman, Superman, Mickey Mouse and Tarzan.

Tarzan came from the fertile imagination of Edgar Rice Burroughs. He started writing when he was thirty-five and wrote seventy-eight stories, including twenty-six Tarzan books, eleven Mars books, five Venus books, seven Earth's core books, four western books and twenty-six non-series books – plus two other non-fiction booklets. The success of his books and movies from the books made ERB enough gold to purchase a 450-acre ranch in the San Fernando Valley just north of Hollywood. That ranch is now in the city of Tarzana.

I know I would have liked Edgar a lot.

Not a bad track record for a failed pencil sharpener salesman.

I had a bunch of heroes while I was growing up. Come to think of it, at seventy I'm still growing up and still have many of the same heroes. Tarzan was right up there with many athletes... Jackie Robinson, Stan Musial, Senator Bill Bradley of the New York Knicks, Goose Tatum of the Harlem Globetrotters, and many more, too many to mention. My dad and my granddad were my biggest heroes.

Johnny Weismuller was starring as Tarzan in my youth. He was one of many athletes to play the role. He had won four Olympic gold medals for swimming.

If you are planning to play the role of Tarzan, here are a few helpful hints I'll share with you that will save you pain and maybe your life. I know they came in handy when I was playing "King of The Jungle."

As far as I know, African elephants, the ones with big floppy ears, are difficult to train. The elephants that I rode were Indian. They are very trainable, but Tarzan lives in Africa so they had to strap on fake African ears. This is a good thing. The rubber ears look very

Get Danton Burroughs to do the yell.

20

realistic and the audience will think they're African. But the best thing about them is that you will have a strap to hang onto when you are up there. And you are "up there." They don't make short elephants.

Another elephant riding tip: elephant hair is like a wire brush. A loincloth isn't much of a cushion. And when an elephant stops walking he doesn't stop moving. All four feet are planted but they continually rock back and forth. So ask for a small rug to sit on, the same gray color as the elephant.

Skinny? When I was a kid I was so skinny I didn't have a shadow. I was thinner than that guy on the inside back cover of comic books. The guy that was always getting sand kicked in his face by the well-built beach bully, in the Charles Atlas advertisements for his course in Dynamic Tension, guaranteed to make a man out of you.

In ninth grade, two buddies and I were walking down a street to the beach to get sand kicked in our faces. We saw a guy walking across his front yard holding a potted palm tree at arm's length. The tree had to weigh one hundred and fifty pounds. This guy was at least fifty years old. He had a little gray at his temples. He was wearing a bathing suit and he was put together, built. He said "Hello, fellas." We stopped to chat. The sand in the face could wait.

Turned out he was Charles Atlas. We thought the guy was a myth. Not! What a guy!

When I got home that evening, still wiping sand out of my face, I asked Dad to buy me a set of weights. I was five feet eleven inches tall, and weighed one hundred and nineteen pounds at that time. That was with rocks in my pockets. Dad bought me a one hundred and five pound set of weights and I made a workout room in the basement.

I still exercise. Not heavy weights. Never been a body builder. I just worked out to make me a better athlete and now I work out to be as independent as I can be. I still get around on my own. It works. Exercise to live, not live to exercise. The point is, if you want to monkey around in life, have more fun, get in shape.

The Tarzan yell? The best rendition I have heard is Carol Burnett's. Make that the second. The best at it is Danton Burroughs, Edgar Rice Burroughs' grandson. Figures. He grew up with it.

MGM gave me a tape of the yell, weeks before we started filming, so I could rehearse. I was living in Venice Beach at the time. After dark I would go down to the water's edge and yell. I didn't get arrested because the surf blotted out my yells. I never came close. At best, I sounded more like a wounded yak. When they edited the film, they cut out my miserable attempts and lay in the recording.

The closest I get to the sound is while slowly lowering myself into a bathtub full of ice cubes. Not worth it. So when you get the part of Tarzan, get Carol or Danton or the record.

Here's another tip. Once you've played the role, everyone will want you to do the yell, especially kids. I tell them I can't do it because if I do, ALL the animals for miles around will come here and the police and zoo people wouldn't like that. Most of the kids go away thinking I am a fake.

Hanging on to the rubber strap that holds the rubber ears in place.

CHAPTER 31
I'M A TENDERFOOT

I have big feet. I wear size fourteen B shoes. Dad said I have a "good understanding."

Back in the fifties, there was a professional wrestler named Antonio Rocca. He was really agile. He wrestled barefoot. The soles of his feet were tougher than leather. He was born in Sicily and didn't have shoes until he was about twenty. I bet he could walk on broken glass.

On the other foot, I wore shoes at the beach and everywhere else. When I got a grain of sand in my shoe I had to stop, take off my shoe and my sock and get rid of that sand. You've heard of the play, "The Princess and The Pea?" When I got the role of Tarzan, I turned into the "The King of The Jungle and The Grain of Sand".

The sound stage is not a good place for bare "poodies!" Some of the trees are made of cement. The wooden floor is torn up from so many nail holes it looks like shredded wheat and there are double headed nails all over the place. They are left there by the crew that took down the last set.

You've never seen a Tarzan with Hush Puppies on. Not even sneakers or thongs or slippers. They just don't fit the part. There was one Tarzan who always wore knee-length suede boots. He looked more like Frank Buck than Tarzan.

To cut down on my, "OW – EEE – OOS," the make-up department made some rubber soles to glue on. They took a mold of my feet, filled the mold with a gooey rubber or plastic mix and there they were – my footprints, kinda like those clowns that make molds of "Bigfoot's" prints in the snow.

They trimmed off the ragged edges and they looked like skin-colored "Odor Eaters." They glued them on the bottom of my feet and they felt great. When I was standing you couldn't see them, and they even put a little bounce in my walk.

My footprints (odor eaters) were just behind me... Footprints in the sand.

For the very first shot of the filming, one of the prop men set up a ten-foot ladder right in back of the camera. I was to swing off the ladder, over the camera and let go of the vine (the vines were rope covered with moss and a leaf or two). When I let go of the vine, I'd drop to the ground right in front of the camera, while the camera shot the scene over my shoulder. Jane and her father were to run straight at me, and the camera.

It was Tarzan to the rescue. I was going to save them from a stampede. The stampede was film from another movie. I think they used footage from "King Solomon's Mines," starring Stewart Granger.

That's the way Hollywood film producers save money. To shoot a stampede would be very expensive. Why not call a film library and rent a stampede that's already been shot?

"Hello, can I rent one Gazelle stampede, fifty feet of film of birds taking flight from a jungle, preferably pink flamingos and three minutes of underwater shots of alligators? All in color."

They call it, "stock footage." At least twenty percent of this Tarzan film would turn out to be stock shots. They even rented black and white film and tinted it green to match their color film. After taking great pains and almost no money to match it up with their color film, it turned out to look like black and white film, tinted green.

Spirits were high on the first day. The first shot, and everyone was ready. Jane's blouse was appropriately ripped. Her father, played by Robert Douglas, had just the right amount of make-up sweat and dirt on his clothes and face.

I had been covered with "Negro #1" pancake make-up - a glorious color. It had taken an hour and a half to put on. Then they rubbed a layer of VO-5 hair oil on top of the make-up to make me glisten. It took another hour and a half to wash it all off each night.

"Camera – Action!"

Jane and her father run toward the camera and I swing from the top of the ladder over the camera and drop from the sky right on my marks. My momentum makes me hop forward about two feet, like those vaulters do in gymnastics when they fly off the pommel horse.

One small hop for Tarzan.

No great leap for man's soles.

Footprints in the sand. My custom odor eaters were right back where I had first landed. That was the first and last time they were used.

# CHAPTER 32
GATOR AID

Tarzan films are not known for their "love scenes." Maybe the chimps hold hands or the hippos do a little water nuzzling, but that's about it.

The love scene was scheduled for after lunch. Good. The MGM commissary had great spaghetti on Tuesdays. I'd have a big plate. That's because I know the love scene goes like this in the script: "Tarzan climbs out of the river and grabs Jane by the ankle and tickles her foot." That's it.

Then they cut to the baby elephant and I go over to the elephant. Cut. Then the prop man tapes a hose to the back of my hand and it looks like I am squirting Jane using the elephant's trunk.

No one ever confused Tarzan with any character Errol Flynn or Cary Grant played. You couldn't pay them enough.

I'm very full of a nice Italian lunch and they give me the news there has been a slight change. The alligator fight scene is next. Oh boy! They're using a twenty-five year old mechanized gator. It is twenty-five feet long and looks believable. One catch: it hasn't been used in a quarter of a century and the motor doesn't work. So they tie a wire to its snout and pull it across the river.

The prop man floats it back so they can pull it right toward the camera. I'll swim in from camera right and meet it mid-stream and the fight begins.

I put the rubber knife in my mouth, wade to my mark – a lily pad they've anchored in place – and the director directs. I haven't gone

> "No one ever confused Tarzan with any character Errol Flynn or Cary Grant played. You couldn't pay them enough."

four strokes when my lunch tells me it's not going along for the ride. So I slow down, let the gator pass. I swim around the bend and feed the fish.

Everyone is yelling at me. They think I hadn't seen the gator go by. When the assistant director runs around the bushes on the shore, he can see I'm not feeling too good and lets

This is as sexy as it gets.

the others know.

I'm ready now. Let's go right away; the gator is back, I'm back, take two.

Just before we meet, I dive to the bottom. It's only four-feet deep. I grab the knife and push off the bottom with both feet. I surface like a skinny whale and land on top of the gator's head... splish, splash and a stab here and there. I give it all I have, which isn't much. But I don't want to do it again so I keep going until I'm all tuckered out.

When I stand up and look to shore the whole cast and crew are on laughing gas. They're staggering around slapping each other on the back. Some are falling down from laughing so hard. Wading to the camera I ask to be let in on the joke.

It seems that when I came down on the gator's head he was so old and stiff his tail came up out of the water and he sank like a leather submarine.

They used stock footage of a gator fight that Johnny Weissmuller did twenty-five years earlier with the same alligator, when the darn gator's machinery was working. It was a terrific fight scene, realistic. It was in black and white. No sweat. They tinted it green. It matched the green of my face.

CHAPTER 33
IT'S A JUNGLE OUT THERE

Animal crackers. Not the tasteless ones I used to eat by the thousands. I'm thinking about the times animals make us crack up. The things that animals do with us or to us that make us giggle, snicker, and laugh out loud—crack up.

Playing the role of Tarzan is like being in a zoo. Chimps and elephants, lions and tigers and bears, oh my, are in your neighborhood. Well, not tigers and bears. They are in the Indian neighborhood, not African. Snakes and hippos and zebras too, but in our production, they were stock footage. We couldn't afford the real thing.

A chimp's DNA is ninety-eight percent the same as ours. Smart? You bet, and strong. But then human hands and arms would be as strong if we walked on them like chimps do.

They can be dangerous, as they get older. Ask Mike Henry about that. A chimp bit him on the chin during the filming of a Tarzan movie. He only got sixty-seven stitches. Mike said he noticed the nibble right away.

The chimp on our show seemed docile but the trainer warned me up front, "If he bites you, punch him in the nose."

One scene was about the chimp running up to Tarzan, grabbing his hand (my hand) and pulling Tarzan back in the direction of the camera, all this to save Jane for the umpteenth time.

To get the shot, the chimp trainer stood behind the camera; I was in front, walking away. "Action!"

The trainer commands, "Go get him!" The chimp runs in and grabs my hand. "Bring him here!" yells the chimps' boss. I resist because I'm angry with Jane, a lovers' spat.

Now what's the chimp to do? This hairless clown won't let him obey his trainer's command. I felt his teeth sinking into the meat of my left hand. I lifted my hand and the chimp came with it. A right cross to his nose and I saved a chunk of my hand from becoming chimp lunch. It took a long time to get the chimp to grab my hand again. It didn't take a long time once he grabbed it for me to turn around and go with him, back to his trainer and friend.

Jane (Joanna Barnes), the "white hunter" (Cesare Denova), the chimp and I were riding through the jungle, toward the camera. I was first. No, the chimp was cradled in my left arm, and Jane was right behind me holding on to my latissimus dorsi, and Cesare was last.

It had taken forty-five minutes to get everyone in place. We each had to climb a ladder and get settled up there, and then one elephant trainer stood in front of the gray mountain and fed him some straw, while the other trainer came up the ladder and handed the chimp to me. This particular elephant didn't enjoy chimps riding on his back. That was our reason for being so sneaky.

We heard "Action!" filter through the plastic jungle. The camera was forty yards down the trail. The trainer yelled whatever you yell at elephants to make them go and we were off at two miles per hour.

We hadn't gone far when I heard Jane (Joanna) cursing. She could say anything she wanted as long as she stayed behind me. There was no dialogue so the microphones were off but it would ruin the shot if the camera picked up her mouth moving.

This is what I heard, "Stop this #*>#*^~+\\<~#!" The problem? The chimp was reaching under my arm and with his extremely long arm could reach certain parts of Joanna's anatomy. He seemed to enjoy squeezing.

The way I was holding the chimp, his mouth was in range of my chin, and my right hand was busy holding onto the strap that held the rubber African ears in place. So I did nothing to stop the chimp's explorations.

The more important problem was not to crack up. A laughing Tarzan in this time of peril in the script would not do. So I bit my own lip. Joanna did not enjoy the stroll.

The elephant was big. He was taller than

> **"The chimp... with his extremely long arm could reach certain parts of Joanna's anatomy."**

I when he was lying on his side. That's where he was in this scene. He had been shot by a poison arrow and the trainer got him in position so I could pull the arrow out, turn and show Jane and the hunter why the elephant was headed for the "elephant burial ground."

The prop department had made a rubber socket to put the arrow in. The socket had a rubber border about ten inches in diameter. It was thin and looked like the skin of the elephant and it allowed the socket to be glued on the side of the elephant. Insert the arrow and it would stay there until I pulled it out. The prop man warned me to put my left hand flat against the border and press down while I pulled the arrow out. Otherwise the whole thing, the socket and its rubber border, would come unglued and ruin the shot.

"Action!" I pushed down firmly on the border glued on to the elephant's stomach. Do you know the difference between a cocktail lounge and an elephant's fart? One is a bar room and one is a BAHHHROOOM!

The show must go on. I turned to show the arrow to Joanna and Cesare. They were gone. The camera operator was gone, along with the director and the rest of the crew. Crack up!

I swear to you, the elephant does have rubber ears!

25

Believe me, it is a guava!

CHAPTER 34
UP THE RIVER

Dad was a Phi Beta Kappa. Joanna Barnes was too. No wonder the role of Jane in a Tarzan flick wasn't much of a challenge for her. She would arrive at the MGM set carrying a thick stack of reading material. It took both her hands to carry it.

I was voted "class clown" of my graduating class at University High in West Los Angeles. The stack of books I brought each day anyone could carry with no hands.

We had a fight scene in the tree house. It wasn't really a fight scene; more like a tussle. Tarzan had carried Jane there while she was out cold. She comes to in this strange place, with this strange creature leaning over her and she flips, loses her composure. We do a little dance of trying to calm her panic and the scene ends with me making her a peace offering of papaya.

In the rehearsal, Joanna slaps me in the face. She wasn't really mad at me. She was doing what the script called for. Now, being a devout coward and not being drawn to anything resembling pain, the slap got my attention.

> "Now, being a devout coward and not being drawn to anything resembling pain, the slap got my attention."

The next rehearsal I was ready and I'm glad I was. I caught her hand just before it landed. The director liked what he saw and said, "Let's shoot it."

Our make-up was checked. When your whole body is covered with make-up there's lots of places to check. Let's do it. "Action!"

Here comes the slap. I caught her right wrist and was feeling rather smug when, out of the corner of my eye, here comes her left hand. I caught it too but it was fear and pure luck. I was down on one knee and my other knee was in front of her, between her captured hands. She bit it. My knee! She bit it.

That hurt. I'm perturbed (mad). I kinda threw her into the corner of the bamboo room. Let me correct that, I didn't kinda – I threw her. "Cut!" yelled the director. "Print it."

We had done it in one take. Joanna and I never discussed the scene. I don't know if she called it method acting. I do know it made the tussle more believable, more real. Why wouldn't it? It WAS real. I'll have to ask her some day.

> **"It's a quiet, romantic scene. One problem – Joanna's teeth are chattering so loud you can't hear her lines. They forgot to heat the water."**

On the back lot at MGM, there was a cement river basin they had built to shoot Johnny Weissmuller in his Tarzan films. He starred in twelve Tarzan films - far more than anyone else. He was my film hero. He was my Olympic hero. "Twice The Hero," is the title of a book written by David Fury about Johnny Weissmuler. If you like real hero stories, read it.

Joanna and I were to float gently down this river among beautiful lily pads and flowers while she spoke a monologue. She is talking to herself more than to Tarzan... wondering aloud what he was all about; how this strange man came to be here and what he thinks of her.

It's a quiet, romantic scene. One problem – Joanna's teeth are chattering so loud you can't hear her lines. They forgot to heat the water. I didn't have any lines so I could grit my teeth. Poor Joanna. She sounded like a very pretty typewriter.

After several takes, someone suggested a solution... brandy. That would warm her up. It did. But now there was a different problem. Call it giddy, or maybe tipsy is a better name. She was intoxicated. She was having so much fun that I was tempted to take a swig.

After a few cups of coffee, she performed wonderfully. Method acting or not, it worked. It took an hour and five wool blankets for me to warm up.

26

This was a nice way to freeze to death.

CHAPTER 35
CAT'S ME-OW

What's the thirty foot fence for? And why the guy with the rifle? I wanted to know. The day was starting out strange enough to ask a few questions. Got the usual hour and a half all over make-up on, and the loincloth fit fine after the river scene the day before.

Joe Newman, the director, says, "I have a lady I want you to meet." He motioned to where a nice little gray haired lady was sitting. This lady was the perfect casting for "The little old lady from Pasadena" who owned the used car you're interested in buying. She had a sweet smile on her face, was well groomed, with a smooth voice, and a full-grown cheetah at her feet. She had a full-grown cheetah, the fastest land animal in the world, for a house pet.

It was a beautiful animal. It was on a leash and had a full muzzle over its face. "Go ahead, give it a pat," Joe chortled. "She won't hurt you. We want you to jump down off that limb," he said, pointing to a ten foot high cement tree limb above the jungle trail set, " and roll around on the ground with Mrs. Spencer's kitty here."

The fence and the guy with the rifle started to make sense. Now Momma didn't have no stupid children so I suggest, "Let George do it." George was my stunt double.

> "Now Momma didn't have no stupid children so I suggest, 'Let George do it.' George was my stunt double."

"George called in sick so Tom here will be your double today." "Hi Tom," I say. "I'd sure...

"There's no danger. This kitty is a love," purrs Director Joe.

"I'd like to see Tom jump on her first," I said, a little more forcefully. "But..." "No Joe!" I cut him off, "Tom first—then me."

Now this stunt is not a simple one. First they lead the cat out the door so it won't see Tom climb up on the limb. Then a guy takes a live goose out of a cage around the corner of the sound stage. When he comes around the corner with that goose flapping its wings he has the full attention of our kitty. The guy backs through the stage door holding the goose

The "paws that defleshes."

up in front of the cat that is putting a strain on its leash.

Once on the set, the goose handler drags the goose along the jungle trail right under Tom. The cat handler takes kitty a few steps the opposite direction. It's working. The cat is zoomed in on lunch and the goose is very concerned.

Joe tugs on the shirt of the camera operator and it's rolling. The handler releases the cat and it hunkers down in a slow motion stalking mode. She's headed down the trail, right under Tom. Everybody holds his breath.

Tom starts to crouch. He moves about two inches. The cat heard him and she's gone. "Cut!"

It wasn't Tom's fault. Cats have 20/20 ears. Now we have a problem. The cat won't go under the limb, not with Tom up there. An hour later the handlers still have the same problem.

This is a low, very low, budget film. Time is costly so the director takes a short cut. "Denny you get in there with the cat and roll around on the ground with her."

"I'd like to see Tom do it first" I suggest. No, I command! I'm thinking George, my regular double, isn't sick. He's just smart. He's got the guts of a Toreador and he wants no part of this stunt. If he won't, I'm not stepping inside that 30-foot fence.

The handlers brought in kitty and let Tom play with her. The cat rolls on its back and plays footsy with Tom. The leash is taken off and the camera rolls. This is not working. The cat looks as threatening as a kid's tabby.

Tom gives her a little slap on the nose. There's a blur, the cat is gone and Tom is standing there bleeding from a claw cut that goes from his shoulder, down his chest, down his loincloth and his thigh to his knee.

After they coax kitty with some tidbits and get her leash back on, she's off the set and out on the street. And Tom's off to the nearest hospital. They gave me a rubber knife and a stuffed leopard doll. Just like I did with the rubber alligator, I vanquish the doll in a brave and ferocious manner. That means I roll around in the grass pretending to stab tabby with my rubber knife.

It has to be one of the funniest scenes in the film. Awful!

Tom survived. I never saw him again and George showed up the next day in perfect health.

I was reminded of one of Mel Brooks' lines about war. "Run, run, run away and live to fight another day!" Besides, cats make me sneeze.

CHAPTER 36
TWO SPECIAL ARTISTS

DUM-DUM. I'm not talking about singing along when you know the tune but don't know the lyrics. I'm not stuttering about the state of someone's brain. I AM talking about the sound of the jungle drums in Edgar Rice Burroughs' Tarzan stories. They call the natives together.

The 2003 gathering was held in Louisville, Kentucky. The Burroughs Bibliophiles came from all over the jungle. Natives blew in from all points of the world. Two came from Vienna, Austria, one from London and the rest were from all over the United States and Canada.

George T. McWhorter was the host. He's hosted more meetings than any other native. Why? He has the world's largest, most complete Burroughs collection. And he's unrivaled as a host.

I've attended many Dum-Dum's. As an X Tarzan, I have a lifetime pass. They are great fun, these fans of ERB. Among them you'll find serious book collectors, movie buffs, toy collectors, authors of books about the men who have played the role of Tarzan on film, and artists who have illustrated the book covers and the posters and the lobby cards and the calendars for ERB stories.

Boris Vallejo and his wife Julie Bell are two of the most famous and talented of these artists. They were the guests of honor this year.

Their fans knew Julie and Boris were going to attend the Dum-Dum. So many of them brought artwork for them to sign.

The waiting line stretched for yards across the huge room.

I've been to a lot of these fan conventions. I've watched big-name stars from Steve Allen to Buddy Hackett, Don Knotts, Bruce Bennett, Anne Francis and others to see how

Boris Vallejo and Julie Bell.

117

they receive this out-pouring of adoration from their fans.

Some make it an assembly line experience for the fan. The star very seldom makes eye contact with the adoring fan. The star keeps signing their photographs, head down, ignoring the excitement, the pure joy that they are being bathed in.

Other stars and artists take the time to let the walls down, open themselves to this strange ritual. They talk with each fan. They are sincere in their "thank you's." After all, these admirers have wept and laughed and been entertained for years by these actors and artists. The fans are showing their gratefulness, and yes, even their love by giving the star money for an autographed photo or illustration.

I could see Julie and Boris appreciated it. They appreciated this aura, this kindness – a gift, a tribute from their fans.

Have you ever seen or talked with people that are completely comfortable in their skin? They are satisfied with who they are. They have easy access and welcome you into their world. The password is, "Hello." Julie and Boris are like that.

Their art shows the human body as the Greeks saw it in their Golden Age. Julie and Boris have developed their muscles. The layman calls it bodybuilding. It's a very simple

Julie's beautiful reality.

Out there on the cutting edge with Boris.

process. A muscle grows when you make it work harder than the day before. The next day you work other muscles, while you rest the ones you worked today. You feed the muscle groups nourishing food and they will become stronger, bigger and more defined. The key word here is WORK. Let me correct that. HARD WORK.

In their illustrations, they present the human body in the beauty that it can be. They capture perfectly-developed men and women in action, or poised to spring into action. We admire these humans as *fantasy*. But Boris and Julie know they are real. They have lived in that world.

I had the pleasure of sharing a meal with them at the Dum Dum. I have a degree in kinesiology from UCLA. Physical education is what that word means. It's the study of muscles and how they move us through our lives. For years I have signed my letters "Stay healthy." I want to remind people I care about to take care of themselves. After just a few minutes with Julie and Boris, I could tell they don't need reminding. The world they live in reflects the world they create with their art. It's a healthy world and because of that, a world with much beauty.

28

Me Tarzan, she Jane, you King Hussein.

CHAPTER 37
TWO KINGS AND A QUEEN

One of the most ignored signs in Hollywood was and still is:

CLOSED SET
No visitors

It's usually placed on the door of the sound stage the production company is filming on. It's always in bold red print on a white background. It's placed at about average eye-level, so it's really hard to miss.

Sometimes the director requests it. Sometime a star actor wants it. Peter Sellers, when he was filming "The Party" had the sign put up. He also requested that no one on the set wear purple. No one knew why but did as requested. After all, he was a comic genius. He didn't complain when Andy Williams came to visit Claudine Longet.

When a nude scene is scheduled, the sign is most often ignored. Now I'm talking about the small entrance... the one that all sound stages have where it's a squeeze for two people to use at the same time.

There is another stage door. This one is a double door. It's thirty to forty feet wide and forty feet high, at least. It is used to move potted trees and backdrops and cars and trucks and skip loaders that haul the other stuff. You can drive a tank or an eighteen-wheeler through these doors with room to spare. These doors are kept closed most of the time during the day. The set crews use them at night to remove the set that was filmed that day and bring in walls and plants and furniture and lights to build the set for the next day's shooting.

In 1959, we were filming a scene on the jungle set when these doors opened and in drove at least twenty Los Angeles police on motorcycles. They were grouped around a shiny black stretch limo with little flags on the front fenders. The police parked their cycles and dismounted. They were the biggest cops, the tallest I'd ever seen. I was barefooted, but I'm six-foot four-inches tall, and they all towered over me.

One of them opened the back door to the limo and out stepped a nice looking man in a suit that must have cost more than I made for the whole film. The man was King Hussein, of Jordan.

The cast was introduced, the director and a few others. Joanna and I got to shake his hand and I got his autograph. Hey, I was just "King for a Day"—king of a plastic jungle. He was king of a whole country for the rest of his life.

We exchanged a few pleasantries. Like, "This is my bamboo house and that's my chimp, well, not really mine." When it comes to making small talk with kings, I get very small. He explained he was on a tight schedule, popped back in his limo and he and the giant cops were off. The visit took maybe ten minutes. Time flies when you're goofing off with a king.

Nobody told him it was a CLOSED SET.

Dr. Onel T. Linn, my granddad, visited us another day. I spent so many summers with him and my grandmother that, as a kid, I called them Momma Ruth and Daddy Doc.

Doc was getting up there in age. So he came in his wheelchair. When he saw me in my outfit in our little chunk of jungle – well the look in his eyes made me feel like a real king. I'll remember his hug and that look all my life. It makes me warm right now.

My grandparents, Dr. Onel "Doc" and Ruth Linn.

CHAPTER 38
PETER SELLERS WAS A GENIUS

Run for cover. That's what I do when I hear "Let's party!" I'd rather take a walk, read a book, get some exercise, have a snack or do nothing. Parties don't interest me at all.

Except one party. I go to it once or twice a year. I sit in the dark, with friends or by myself, and always have fun. Peter Sellers is there. It's really his party.

A genius is a person who possesses exceptional creative powers. Peter Sellers was a comic genius. We are very fortunate that his movies will always be available so that we can delight in his genius. "The Party" is just one of many packages of laughter that make up his legacy.

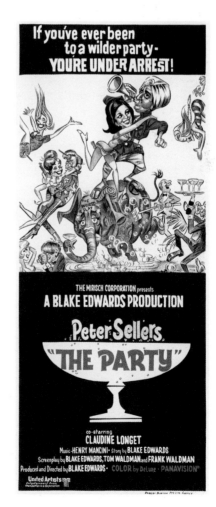

The movie took twelve weeks and one day to shoot. A small group of actors were privileged to go along for the ride. For me, it was the most exciting job I ever had. It wasn't a job. It was a dream. I guess working / playing with a genius can be otherworldly. I know I couldn't wait to get to the studio every morning.

Blake Edwards produced and directed it. He did all the Pink Panther films. If it hadn't been for Blake's confidence and the safe atmosphere he created for all us supporting actors, "The Party" couldn't have been created.

I say "created" because that's what happened. The script was only forty pages long. One hundred and twenty or more pages is the usual length for a movie script. So Blake and Peter made the whole thing up as they went along.

The whole cast signed contracts requiring them to be on stage every morning at eight. Why? Because nobody, not even Blake, knew which actors would be needed to work. When you don't have a road map you have to load up all kinds of tires.

Blake would start each scene by gathering the actors he wanted in the scene. Then he'd give us a description of the

29

It's a "gotcha!"

scene:

"You're teaching this French beauty how to play pool. But you're really just using that as a ploy to grope her. Along comes Peter and he recognizes you as Wyoming Bill Kelso, one of his TV cowboy heroes back in India."

Then he would say "Action!" And off we'd go into unchartered territory. There would be no rehearsal, no script – none of us knew where we were going or where we'd end up. What Blake was saying to us was "Have courage – wing it – let this genius take you where you've never been – have fun - I'll catch you if you fall."

Blake would say "cut" when he wanted, except for one scene when he was quietly laughing so hard he couldn't say cut. We found him under the dinner table on his back, out of breath. The assistant director yelled cut.

Blake had asked for a videotape camera to be mounted on top of the film camera. Up to that time only Jerry Lewis had used this technique.

After every scene was filmed, Blake and Peter would go into a small enclosure that had been built on the stage and they'd watch an "instant replay" of the scene. If we heard laughter from them, we knew we'd go on to the next scene, whatever that was. If there was no laughter we knew we'd do the same scene over only differently.

Exciting? When you see actors on a film set watching other actors work; when you know those same actors aren't needed for the scene being shot, you know something extraordinary is going on. That's how wonderful it was to watch a genius create. He made better actors of us all.

I think we were all sad when the twelve weeks came to an end. The wrap party was low key. Blake brought his wife, Julie Andrews. To meet her was to relive "The Sound of Music." Goodbyes lasted two weeks. Then my agent called and said I was needed for one day of retakes.

> "Then he would say 'Action!' And off we'd go into unchartered territory. There would be no rehearsal, no script – none of us knew where we were going or where we'd end up."

This would be the only time the actors knew where the scenes were going. We would be free to take a different route, but we knew the end of the scene had to match.

I had a week to think about what I could do to have my character surprise Peter. I had a friend take a picture of me on Horseback wearing my Wyoming Bill Kelso tux. Thirty-five years later I still have that tux. Wyoming Bill was such a delightful jerk. Only a jerk would have his name embroidered on the back of his tux.

I had a copy of the photo made the size of a post-card, the kind some TV and movie stars give to fans. Then I got a ticket, an old ticket to some long past event. When they did the retakes of the scene in the game room where Peters' character recognizes Wyoming, I'd spring these surprises on Peter from my tux pocket.

Peter had a history of breaking up during the shooting of a scene. Remember at the end of his film "Being There," when they roll credits over out-takes of Peter laughing uncontrollably?

Well, halfway through the retake of the pool table scene Peter giggled. The next take he got halfway to halfway and lost it. On take twenty- seven, when Blake yelled "action," we could hear Peter laughing off stage.

Blake called, "lunch!" We broke for two hours. When we came back, Peter had his act together. He went through the scene with ease. He never said a word about what had set him off. He never mentioned it.

I still hope, over a quarter of a century later, it was my silly photo of Wyoming Bill Kelso that I sprung on him that made him be consumed by laughter. I will want to believe that the rest of my life.

Listening to Blake Edwards' suggestions.

We having fun yet? Not many folks have a butterfly on their tux sleeve.

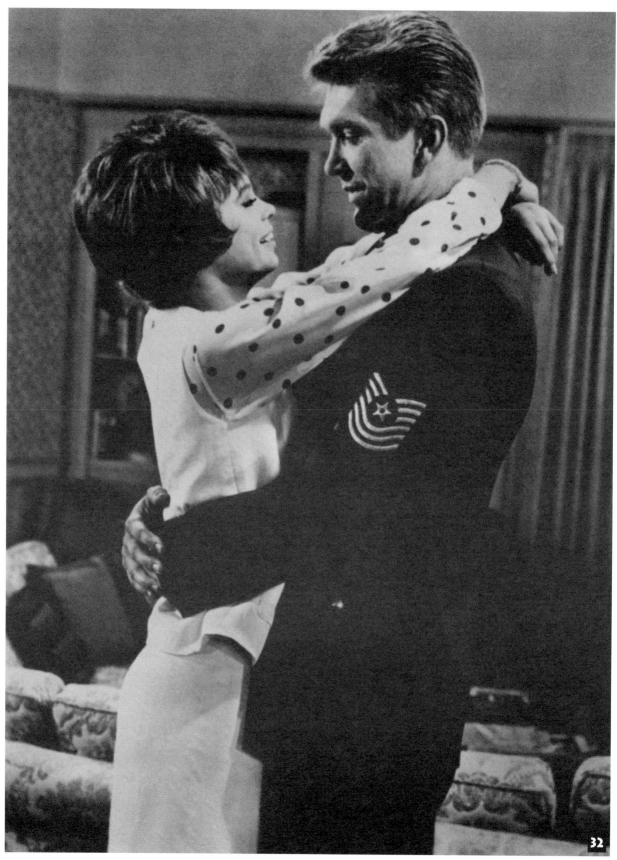

Juliet Prowse and me.

CHAPTER 39
LEGS

Legs are good. Well, some legs are. I like legs. Chicken legs are up there on my list, right next to turkey legs. I'm not much interested in any other animal legs. Horse legs seem too skinny for all that weight and speed. You can tell I'm not a real cowboy. Dogs' legs are usually too hairy to get a good look at. Turtle legs are special. Retractable, that's special.

Human legs get my full attention. I look with envy at a trackman's legs - muscular, limber, well formed from ankle to hip, built for speed and jumping and vaulting. I've accused God of putting my legs on backwards. How can I be bow-legged, knock-kneed and have knobby knees all at the same time and not have my legs on backwards? On top of that, or I should say on the bottom of that, my feet are three sizes too big for my body and I'm pigeon-toed. People have told me I walk around with my nose in the air. It's just to avoid looking down.

Ladies' legs, gams, stems, wheels – long, shapely dancers' legs can be a distraction. They have caused me much pain. I've walked into lampposts, walls, other people, almost everything you can name while ogling at a pair of beautiful legs.

Juliet Prowse. Does that name bring the vision of the Olympics of legs? I had to play her husband in a TV series called "Mona McClusky" created by writer, producer, actor, and director Don McGuire. He also wrote the classic film about prejudice, "Bad Day at Black Rock" and the original script for "Tootsie."

I know playing Juliet's husband in a sitcom for twenty-six weeks was a dirty job but somebody... Any way, the first day of rehearsal for the pilot arrived. The cast was there; Juliet and me and Elena Verdugo and Robert Strauss who played "Animal" in "Stalag 17", and Herb Rudly.

The cameraman was there with his assistants. Roy Stork from make-up was there. Interesting guy, he had been on the "Dolittle Raid" in WWII. The prop department was well represented along with the sound department and the grips.

We were seated at a long table in the middle of a large sound stage. Two rather harsh lights provided enough light for everyone to read their scripts and take notes. This oval of bright light dropped off in all directions so the group was surrounded by darkness.

No Mr. Don Mcguire, our director/producer and leader. Five minutes went by, ten minutes – he was ten minutes late. People began to fidget in their seats.

The stage door opened off in the darkness and let a streak of light slice the black in two. We could see Don's silhouette in the doorway. The door closed behind him and he disappeared. We could hear his footsteps. He was in no hurry. He walked into our light and everyone sat up to greet him and begin.

He walked right by us. No hello, no nod. It was as if we didn't exist. And he walked into the dark beyond. We heard him stop and out of the silence... "Fudge!!!!!!!!!!!!!!" It bounced off the walls and us.

Don appeared out of the darkness with a big smile on his face.

"Now we can get started."

Don was like that. He used humor, which is based on surprise, to break the tensions in life. I miss him very much.

For twenty-six weeks it was a joy to come to work. George Burns. Right, the one and only George Burns, took over as producer. Richard Whorf, of the Orson Wells Actors' Group, directed every show. And Robert Strauss, "Animal," kept us laughing from morning till morning.

The show was up against "Thursday Night At The Movies." What a time slot. On our opening night, we were up against "Manchurian Candidate." We could sense the TV audience out there, "What will we watch tonight, Frank Sinatra in a classic film or an $80,000 episode of an unknown sit-com?"

We were ranked sixty-seventh out of sixty-four shows that night and never got any higher. Mom and Dad watched and my brother stood in for me. But everybody in the show had a great time.

We even broke the twin bed barrier for sitcoms. Up until then, even married couples were filmed ONLY in twin beds. I guess when you know your show is going to be cancelled —what the heck, bring on the king-sized bed.

Legs? Juliet danced all over Europe on hers. She danced in Vegas in her own show. She danced in musicals and summer stock all over the U.S. She even danced in the pilot episode for "Mona McClusky." When old guys sit around and praise ladies' legs and no one mentions Juliet Prowse, you know you're with a bunch of amateur leg watchers or old geezers in need of guide dogs.

CHAPTER 40
SURFS DOWN

Face it. Some people like one side of their face better than the other. Tina Louise, who played Ginger on "Gilligan's Island," is one of those people. She had it in her contract that she could only be photographed from one side. Don't know which side. They both looked good to me.

When I was a young sprout I was a photographer. I had a company called, "GOTCHA." I even had a camera. My film subjects were actors and actresses that needed 8x10s for their interviews. Many of them had a favorite side to be photographed from.

I had always thought that my face was symmetrical. Except for a mole on my right cheek, I thought both sides of my face were the same. I would have bet on it.

A lab technician, at the photo lab I took my exposed film to, disagreed. So we set up an experiment. I had recently had most of my hair cut off for the role of a gladiator. It was less than an inch long and combed forward so it looked the same on both sides. I got a photographer friend to photograph my face straight on. The lighting was the same on both sides. I had a black turtleneck sweater on with a black background so that the photo would only show my face.

The film lab man made two 8x10 negatives of the face shot and printed one photocopy. Then he cut the two negatives in half, top to bottom. He took two half negatives of the left side of my face and flipped one over and put the two left sides together. He did the same with the right side and printed a copy of each. It's easy to do, just takes a little time.

The three prints side by side showed three different people – very different people. My face made from two right sides looked like a tough no-nonsense cop. The middle me, the mirror image was my old self. But the face made from two left sides was scary. The face looking back at me was evil. A face only a mummy could love. I wouldn't follow that face down a dark alley. I couldn't introduce that face to a friend and expect to keep the friend. So much for being symmetrical. Tina knew what she was doing.

Gilligan's Island wasn't an island. Well, the pilot was shot in Hawaii but all the other episodes were shot on a sound stage at the corner of Laurel Canyon and Ventura Boulevard in Studio City, in the San Fernando Valley. The lagoon was a cement puddle between the sound stage and the parking lot. Sometimes it's what you don't see that creates the magic of film.

The cast, the writers and the producer provided the other magic in Gilligan's Island. The actors were having a ball. Wouldn't you? Jim Backus called on Mr. Magoo to keep folks smiling. Dawn and Tina were easy on the eye and Bob was Gilligan. Allan Hale, Jr. was really Santa Claus.

Tina and I rehearsed one of our scenes in her dressing room. The room was elegantly decorated with flocked wallpaper and beautiful rugs and antique furniture. I sat down on a one hundred year-old carved chair and broke the back off. Not a good start to the rehearsal.

In the scene it called for Ginger to slap me on the shoulder. The part of Tongo, a poor man's Tarzan, fit the title of the episode, "Our Vines Have Tender Apes." Tongo fainted when he saw animals. I almost fainted the first time Tina slapped me. She really liked that antique chair.

Gilligan's Island has never been off the air. They've been rerunning the show forever. Of the requests I get for photos or autographs, G.I. fans outnumber all the rest.

> **"Tongo fainted when he saw animals. I almost fainted the first time Tina slapped me."**

The part of Duke Williams, a surfer, is a puzzle to most real surfers. They want to know how anyone can surf without a wave. I'm not a surfer and told the producer, up front. He said not to worry, "We have stock footage of a surfer that looks like you surfing a thirty foot wave off Hawaii." "Then we'll cut to you coming across the lagoon on your surfboard. Just hold on to the board and try to stay on your hands and knees." "OK, I can do that."

They drilled a hole in the nose of the surfboard and put a steel bolt through the hole. Then they hooked a cable on the bolt under the board out of sight. The cable went clear across the lagoon, under water, and was attached to a motorized winch on the back of a truck.

I got on the board on the far side of the lagoon. They rolled film... "Action!"

The board got going so fast I thought hey, I bet I could stand up. I did. The board hit the beach so fast I turned a sommersault, stood up, and heard, "Print."

And that's how you surf without a wave. Sometimes it's what you don't see that creates the magic.

Natalie Schafer (Mrs. Howell) and "Tongo" out for a stroll.

34

Clark Kent.

CHAPTER 41
"S" IS FOR SILLY

He's known around the world as a hero. He's looked up to by all kids. He's stronger than anyone, everyone. He's kind to ladies, young and old. He's on the side of the underdog. He can't be killed. And he flies. What better person to tell the youth of America to join the United States Air Force?

Now link that guy with the concept of "Team Effort" and you have a perfect thirty-second Air Force recruiting TV message.

In the spring a young man's fancy turns to baseball. Okay, the love of baseball. And Florida is covered with a migration of the best baseball players in the land. It's called spring training.

I'm going to spend several weeks at ten of these training camps making a one-minute or thirty-second TV recruiting spot at each camp. We'll shoot on the baseball diamond with the players in the background. In the foreground will be that team's manager talking with Superman, me. I get to meet and work with Joe Torre, Yogi Berra, Walter Alston and seven other managers. Plus, I get to meet some of the players.

It was a baseball fan's dream. That was the good news. The not-so-good news was that I have to get dressed and have make-up put on in the team's locker rooms.

Now I've been a jock most of my life. At twenty-six, I'd spent many hours in locker rooms just like these. Basketball teams' locker rooms are the same as baseball locker rooms. The guys are taller in basketball but that's about the only difference.

Just a bunch of young guys, buddies,

With Dodger's manager, Walter Alston.

teammates laughing and scratching, getting ready to spend two or three hours playing a sport that they know they play better than anybody. A bunch of more confident, more outspoken guys is hard to find. Throw a "Hollywood" actor in that pond and watch the fun.

I forgot to mention, being a blond, I had to have a black rinse on my hair each day. There never has been a blond Superman. Tarzan yes, but man of Kryptonite, no! The spring weather in Florida is classified in the category called "sauna/monsoon." A locker room full of fifty sweaty guys is even hotter and muggier. This was not the atmosphere to have a black rinse stay on your hair. I had small black streams running down my forehead and along the bridge of my nose most of the time.

Do you think the players noticed this? Naw! Do you think they made any comments about it? Naw! Nobody threw anything at me except a tidal wave of barbs. I was thankful that it was a baseball team. I was much larger than most of them. If it had been a bunch of NFL teams I may not have survived. I can hear the chorus now, "Superman needs a shower!" As it was, a bystander could tell I wasn't exactly accepted as one of the boys.

It was a long tour of duty. I lost twenty pounds. That was a good thing. And I got to schmooze with the best managers in pro baseball. But as a Superman I felt more like a "Hollywood actor" who took a wrong turn... ten wrong turns.

I apologize to the millions of Superman fans. I was miscast. I know you can find hundreds of ex-baseball players who will agree with me.

CHAPTER 42
FIRE AND ICE

Winter and summer... Michael Green was "winter" and I was "summer." Mike was six-foot seven-inches tall and I was six-feet four-inches. The tiny model town in front of us on a low table was three inches high. That is, the telephone poles were three inches high. The houses were about two inches. The streets had huge cars one-half inch high, traveling up and down.

Mike had snow falling in front of him and I had a huge fire roaring between the town and me.

We were giant trouble for your car. Mike froze engines and I boiled them over. Prestone was the product saving the motorists' day. The TV announcer said, "Don't worry, Prestone will protect you from these two monsters!"

Mike's hair looked like a bird's nest made out of shiny blue ice; a great big Jack Frost with four-inch icy finger nails.

I was painted gold all over. Well, not my head. It was in a gold helmet with pointed gold spikes over a foot long, sticking out in all directions. If the sun had a face on it, I was the sun.

It took over two hours in the make-up chairs to get ready. They even painted my teeth and gums gold. My costume was that of a Roman Centurion complete with the short skirt and chest plate. Everything I touched turned to gold. Eating a sandwich was a real challenge.

One of the make-up men had traveled with Bob Hope all over the world. It's old ski-nose's 100th Birthday as I write this. What an incredible GOOD WILL PACKAGE his life has been. If laughter heals, and I believe it does, Bob Hope has been the most successful doctor of ALL time.

Twenty years ago I was fortunate to be cast as the Texaco Man in one of the many TV spots Mr. Hope did for that company over the years. He had all the lines and he read them from a huge cue card held by the assistant director standing beside the camera.

Bob Hope

137

To read your lines like that and not look to the audience like you're reading takes a great deal of skill. The best actors I've seen do it are Raymond Burr, Marlon Brando and Bob.

When the set was ready - lighting, sound and camera, they called Mr. Hope from his dressing room. He read through the lines three times and the director said, "Give us a few minutes," and Bob went back to his room.

I've done over one hundred and eighty TV spots. The lines an actor is given have been written and re-written for months at the ad agency. They have gone through hundreds of timings. The spot must fit into a thirty-second or sixty-second slot, precisely, to the second. If the actor takes sixty-one seconds to say the lines he's asked to speed it up. If he only takes fifty-eight seconds he's asked to stretch it out. It must be right on time.

They called for Mr. Hope and we filmed the spot. I noticed on the cue card two words had been crossed out. Bob's first readings had been long - just a second or two. They shortened the script. It's good to be "King."

The first year that Prestone aired the winter/summer giants, Mike and I were told they had received phone calls from parents complaining that we "meanies" frightened their children. The second year's spots were even more frightening.

Same little town, same big monsters, but this time they turned up the heat. Mike got to be a blizzard instead of a snowstorm.

Summer? This time instead of just snarling and a little fire licking at the cars they added a fire bolt. I was given an asbestos glove for my right hand. The prop department put a big sheet of glass between me and the camera - to protect the camera and the operator.

They handed me a nurf ball soaked in lighter fluid. I was to throw the ball right at the lens. The ball would be on fire. The effects man explained the step-by-step plan. They would roll camera, he'd light the soaked ball, and I'd hold it at arm's length for a count of three and then zing it at the lens.

The last step and the one that really got my attention, was to dunk my gloved hand in the bucket of water next to my right foot. Why? – The glove would still be on fire. He figured I had five or six seconds from the time the ball left my hand until I started feeling the heat.

I can do that! One, the nurf ball is soaked in lighter fluid. Two, they roll the camera. Three, he lights the ball. WHOOSH! The fluid had dripped through the glove fingers and I didn't wait three seconds to throw the ball. In one second the ball and the glove were ablaze. I let the ball fly and that's when it happened. I was mesmerized. There was a flaring line of fire ten feet long from my fingertips to the glass. It looked as if I could shoot flames out of my fingers. I could not stop watching it. Until I felt a slap on my leg and at the same instant heard, BUCKET! SSSSSSsssssss.

I bet they got a lot of phone calls that next season.

CHAPTER 43
IT'S MILLER TIME

Miller is my name. It's a very common name. Check out the phone book in any large city in the U.S. and you'll see just how common. I think after Jones, Smith and Brown, there are more Millers running around than folks with any other name.

We were headed to Alaska to do a Miller Beer commercial. The four of us were actors and were to depict guys working on the oil pipeline. This was my fourth Miller's TV spot. Other actors accuse me of having a relative high up the corporate ladder at the Miller's company. If I do, it's news to me. But just in case I do have an uncle or cousin working for them... I want him to know I'm available for number five. I don't drink, but I'm not against it.

The first TV ad I did for Miller's was many years ago. At that time they were the only beer in America that came in a clear bottle. Their ads read, "Millers, The Champagne of

12

Bottled Beer." Sales were down so they took a survey and what a surprise they got. No man in his macho mind would order a beer called champagne in the presence of a lady. That wouldn't be manly. Their ad campaign had fizzled.

Their next ads took place in a sports bar, a hangout for jocks. The set of the interior of the bar was built smaller than a real bar. How small? The character I played, "Big Mike" had to duck coming in the door. When I sat I couldn't get my knees under the table. My date was four-foot ten-inches and walked barefooted on the floor. I walked on a wooden runway six inches off the floor. Add to that the fact I was six-feet four-inches with two inch heels. That made me seven-feet tall. The gal came up to my elbow.

The two actors playing the bartenders were five-feet tall and the beer glass they filled for me held three gallons. They passed this huge glass out of frame and then changed it to a regular size glass when it came back in frame to me. This slight of hand made me appear even bigger.

This ad campaign worked. It pays to advertise with the right message. From then on, Miller's TV spots featured pro football players, hockey players, and tough guys, guys that wouldn't be seen drinking champagne on a date. Pipe liners in Alaska fit into that group. We flew to anchorage and then took a 14-passenger plane inland to a hunting lodge. The pipeline wasn't finished, But a section of it went close by the lodge. Ice started forming on the wings of the old plane as we flew low over a huge glacier. Not a good place in sight to land. The pilot opened a window and we had another problem. The exhaust from the two obsolete engines came in. We landed on a muddy field. All of us were part green from the fumes and part white from fear.

We were sixty miles from Valdez, in the warmest southern part of Alaska. It was April. The blizzard that hit us the next morning lasted two days.

The actors stayed in small trailers. The trailers had been divided in half with a paper-thin wall. Each side had a bathroom and a bedroom. The bedroom was so small you had to go outside to change your mind. A twin bed took up so much of the room that when you set your suitcase on the floor next to the bed, there wasn't enough room to open it.

> "The bedroom was so small you had to go outside to change your mind."

For two days the blizzard whistled all round this metal pill. The wind would get under the thing and tip half of it off the ground and then the wind would change direction and let the trailer come down with a bounce. Sleep was impossible.

On the third day the blizzard had passed, but the sky was still overcast. The helicopter that had been reserved for an air shot still couldn't take off. So we were to drive the two-lane road to Valdez and pick up some lumber to build a track for a dolly shot. Doesn't sound like much of an adventure, but it was.

The assistant director stopped to pick us up at 8 a.m., in a three-quarter ton truck. He was drunk. I was the designated driver. The seventy-mile trip to Valdez was slow but uneventful. The local lumberyard had what the director needed. There was time for lunch before we headed back.

Our table at the waterfront café gave us a terrific view of the fishing fleet. Some of the boats were tethered not more than ten feet from us along the low stone wall directly in front of the restaurant. We had a sandwich and fries and the assistant director drank his lunch. It had started to snow and I thought it might be a good idea to get on the road. The A.D. wasn't in a hurry.

Sitting there waiting, I noticed the boats were gone. There hadn't been a fisherman walk by and yet the boats weren't there. They went to sea, mid-day in the snow? I mentioned it to the waitress.

"They're still there," she said smiling. Bad joke, my face said.

"Go see, if you don't believe me."

We went out the front door, across the sidewalk and looked over the three- foot wall. There they were, still moored to the piers. Valdez has a twenty-eight- foot tide. When we turned around the waitress was waving at us through the window.

The first five miles back, the road winds around, climbing out of the harbor. The sign before entering the two-lane tunnel said: "ICY 15 mph". The tunnel has no lights and the walls were solid rock, no cement finish.

Half way through the tunnel, the three-quarter ton truck starts to slide slowly into the oncoming lane. We can see the lights of an approaching vehicle. The next ten seconds are a blur to me. I tried to remember the rules to stop a slide, all the while turning the steering wheel first one way and then the other as I changed my mind from rule to rule.

There was no impact, no jolt, not even a bump. We came to a stop up against the far wall. The oncoming car or truck had missed us or we had missed it. The bad news was we were facing the way we had come, back to Valdez.

The guys were cheering and patting me on the back. "Great driving!" "Way to go!"

"Fantastic man!"

"Not a scratch!"

I didn't have the nerve to tell them I had closed my eyes.

We crept out of the tunnel at three m.p.h. Two guys got out to stop traffic while I tenderly turned the truck around. By now it was snowing big time. They got back in and we tried the tunnel again. Made it. What a relief. We hadn't gone fifty feet and I drove into a "white-out."

I've never been in one before or since. It's like a white sheet dropped on us. You have to stop unless you have a death wish. Like Woody Allen said, "The only way I want to have immortality is by not dying!"

The two guys scrambled out again, one in front and one behind, to stop traffic 'til the thing blew over. By the time we got back to our capsule-shaped trailers I was a nervous wreck.

The bar next to the lodge was a popular place on Saturday night. It was a special Saturday night. The owners were pouring a new cement dance floor. I'm not saying that working on the pipe line was a dull job. I am saying that a lot of people watched cement harden that night. I was one of them.

The company used a local bar by the muddy airfield to do the interior shots for the commercial. They hired local folks as extras to make it look busy, to look like it was a popular place for pipe liners to drink a Miller's.

Several of the extras were attorneys who wanted to see what show biz was like – just slumming. Between shots we all sat around and shot the breeze. I couldn't help but hear a couple of lawyers talking about their recent cases. They kept mentioning, "I had a nine and three Tuesday and I have more next week."

"Excuse me, I don't want to be nosey, but could you tell me what a nine and three is?" One of the lawyers replied, "No problem. That's a divorce that happens when a married couple is snowed in for nine months and out for three. That is, if they don't kill each other first." "It happens so often up here in Alaska we gave it a number."

We finally got the commercial in the can (done). But the director, along with the four actors, didn't want to get back on that collection of rust they laughingly called an airplane. So we rented a car. I was elected the designated driver since I'd saved their lives once, and it was snowing, and I was the only one that didn't drink.

It snowed and it snowed and that night every eighteen-wheeler in Alaska was going the other way on our two-lane road. Every time one passed it was a fight not to be blown off the road. But the hours flew by because of what was going on in the back seat.

The director started a game. "You hum four bars of a song and I'll sing it. Then I'll hum four bars and you'll sing it." You could tell by the tone of his voice he didn't expect to lose this game.

He hadn't counted on Chet. Chet was the actor he had challenged. Chet was a sax player, had his own quartet called "Super Sax," and had recorded several LP's. Surprise.

They played the game for hours all the way to Anchorage. I didn't know there were so many songs. I couldn't believe anyone could remember so many.

I could remember a quote from James Thurber's book, "The 13 Clocks,"

"I can do a score of things that can't be done," the Golux said. "I can find a thing I cannot see and see a thing I cannot find. The first is time, the second is a spot before my eyes. I can feel a thing I cannot touch and touch a thing I cannot feel. The first is sad and sorry, the second is your heart. What would you do without me? Say nothing."

"Nothing," said the Prince.

"Good then you're helpless and I'll help you."

I've known that little morsel for fifty years but I couldn't name you a song from hearing its first four bars to save my life.

What a pleasant drive we had that snowy April night. Alaska is a beautiful place, but I sure wouldn't want to get a nine and three there.

CHAPTER 44
TELL IT TO THE MARINES

I was in the Cub Scouts and the Boy Scouts and the Sea Scouts. The Sea Scouts had great beach parties out of Freeport, Long Island, New York. I never did learn to tie all the complicated knots but sure learned how to party.

On my honor I will do my best
To help the Girl Scouts get undressed
Take what I can and steal the rest

I don't know who taught me that but it sure wasn't the scoutmaster. Maybe the scouts that grew up just a few miles from Brooklyn had a different agenda.

When your family moves about every four years while you're growing up, your mind gets stunted. I know your resident librarian – your memory – takes very long vacations. Dad kept getting better job offers he couldn't refuse. Our family trail went from Indiana to Maryland to Long Island and finally to Westwood, California. Dad really enjoyed teaching at UCLA. He stayed there for over a quarter of a century. So our family has called some part of the Golden State home for more than fifty-three years.

> **"In forty-five years of acting, I've only played two characters out of the Middle Ages."**

Somewhere along the trip, I think it was Silver Springs, Maryland I started getting interested in the Middle Ages. I sat in school and drew pictures of castles and knights in armor. I read books about damsels in distress and watched Errol Flynn in "Robin Hood" save Maid Marian from the bad guys.

In forty-five years of acting, I've only played two characters out of the Middle Ages. One was "Little John", Robin Hood's right-hand man, a character in rags and tights. The other role, the one that took me back to all those drawings of castles and moats with jousting tournaments and sword fights, was that of a medieval king.

143

144

I didn't mean you should really break a leg.

I was to play the White King in a human size chess set. The chessboard was big. Each square was five feet by five feet. The knights were stunt men in armor, on horseback. The horses were real horses wearing fighting armor. All the chess pieces were played by actors... no statues.

It was important that the armor look authentic. It was so important that the producers had an armor specialist flown to California, from London, to make all the armor fit the actors and horses. Even my sword, Excalibur, the legendary sword belonging to King Arthur, had to look just right.

The chessboard was assembled with Vasquez Rocks looming in the background. These rocks are a many layered formation located in the high desert about forty miles north of Hollywood. It has been used for thousands of film productions since the time of Gene Autry westerns. TV shows, movies, commercials and documentaries have been shot with this impressive background. It is also a state park with campgrounds.

We were to work nights for a week. When it got dark, spotlights raked the ominous rocks. The chessboard was rimmed with hundreds of lights shooting straight up. Two forty-foot high propane torches roared between the set and the rocks, making shadows dance on the steep, craggy face.

Misters (fog machines) were used to make a three-foot mist float across the chess set. Wind machines would twirl and spin the mist into a second chess game played by ghosts.

Who has the money to go to all this expense just to make a thirty-second TV spot? The American taxpayer, that's who. This production company was making a recruitment spot for the U.S. Marines.

You may have seen it. It was the one where the medieval warrior magically morphs into a U.S. Marine in dress blues, holding Excalibur at the ready. The Corps used it to recruit for three years.

My brother had been in the Corps. I was in the U.S. Infantry. Kent and I used to compare the training we were given. He had a much tougher course. I don't recommend armor to keep warm. It's kinda like being in a wind tunnel in a refrigerator. Each night the actors would put on another layer of long underwear.

One night it got so cold that the mist froze on the chessboard. Not good for the horses. As chess king, I stood on a round pedestal. It was painted silver just like my armor. The actress playing my queen stood on the rug floor of the chessboard. She was six-foot one-inches tall.

The horse directly in front of the queen and me slipped on the ice. His back hoof went over the edge of the chessboard and hit one of the spotlights, making it explode. The circus was on.

The poor horse was freaked. The armored stuntman tried his best but the horse went down. In all the armor, the stuntman couldn't get his leg out and the horse pinned him there. Now, because of the icy footing, and the rider and the horse's armor, neither of them could get up.

The wranglers came to the rescue. They got the horse up and off the set. But the stuntman couldn't get up. His leg had been broken. Would you believe he was there, in a cast, in his armor, on a different horse the very next night? Those guys are tough, good guys to have in a Marine unit.

Me? I bailed out, jumped down off my wooden base and headed off the chessboard in the direction of my queen. I was quick but not quick enough to catch her. She was a long-legged queen.

When the stuntman had been taken to the hospital and the horse was in his trailer headed for home, I went back to the square section of the chessboard where all the action had happened. There was a six-foot gouge in the rug where the horse's shoe had cut it. The spool-like base I had been standing on was on its side, and eight inches below where my feet had been was a two-inch gash shaped like a hoof. I sighed and thanked the powers that I wasn't a stuntman.

The next night went well. There were no surprises. Well, there was one. About midnight the king felt the "call of nature." So, I walked off into the darkness, in the direction of the campgrounds, and a line of oblong seven-foot sentinels... porta potties.

These were not built for anyone wearing armor; especially a six-foot-four-inch king (I had high armor boots on). I took off my crown and set it on a rock. This closet just wasn't tall enough for crowns.

The troubles I had the next ten minutes could be made into an episode of the English comic, "Mr. Bean." A Cirque du Soleil contortionist comes to mind.

I'd heard hilarious stories of Richard Burton playing Shakespeare. He was known for being able to hold his liquor. But his fellow actors that were also costumed in armor and chain mail, could hear him sloshing by on stage as the play progressed. He also left a damp trail. Apparently, he couldn't hold his drink beyond the first act.

So you can imagine there was an urgency on my part to solve the puzzle of my armor's buckles and clasps. While I was in this Houdini imitation I heard three or four vans drive up and stop nearby. Their passengers spilled out and by their high-pitched voices, I guessed it was a Cub Scout troop earning their camping badge.

I was so busy I didn't care. My priorities were to get out of the tin suit I was wrapped up in. Relief at last. I wouldn't do an impression of Mr. Burton that night.

I took my time reassembling. The kids were unloading their gear and ooing and aahing over the strange spot lighted chess game off in the distance. That's when I made my entrance into their dark world.

I slammed the door open, jumped down the two steps, armor clanking, cape twirling in the breeze, glistening in the moonlight, donned my crown and strode off into the night. There was complete silence. Not even a slosh.

It was freezing.

CHAPTER 45
GO WEST YOUNG MAN

Ojai, California, is seventy-one miles northwest of Los Angeles. I lived there for over twenty years and, when I got an interview or audition for a film or TV job, I'd drive in. On a good traffic day it only took a little over an hour, depending on what part of town the casting call was held in.

Today the call was in Hollywood so I allowed an hour and fifteen minutes. The job was for a TV commercial for a German cigarette called WEST. My agent said I didn't have to be a smoker. That was good, because I'm not.

When I got to the casting agency and signed in, I almost turned around and went home. The ten or twelve guys already there for the part were at least fifteen years younger than me. Since I would have driven one hundred fifty miles round trip, I stuck around even though I figured I wasn't even in the race.

Some guy from the agency came out and divided us up in pairs. They were seeing two guys at a time.

The first pair was called and was in there about five minutes. Me and my new, imaginary buddy were next. The director explained that they were looking for truck driver pals driving an eighteen-wheeler out west. Thus, the name of the cigarette was WEST.

It was pretty close to a Marlboro ad. Their package was red and white. Their truck was going to be red and white. The cowboy was a truck driver and the background would be every red mountain in the west. Southern Utah, Arizona, New Mexico were their planned shooting locations.

The interview – just be yourself in front of the camera and carry on a conversation with your trucker friend. "Roll camera, introduce yourself and action", the director directed. And we were off.

For the next five minutes I turned into a wisecracking, down-home, out-west, good ole boy trucker. I used props off the desk in the room, photos off the walls. That's what I was, off the wall. Didn't figure I had chance for the part so I really hammed it up.

The director cut and we eighteen-wheel truckers headed for the exit. The other fella was a step ahead of me and I felt a hand on my shoulder. I turned and saw it was the director.

"Would you mind staying and doing the interview again? We'll call one actor in at a time and can you do the interview with all of them?" he asked.

All of a sudden my odds for getting a little work seemed to be getting better. I got to do my thing with twenty-one guys - one at a time. They must have had about two hours of tape on me at the end of the day. I didn't repeat my routine. Tried to make it as fresh as I could each time. I had a great time!

> "When I got to the casting agency and signed in, I almost turned around and went home. The ten or twelve guys already there for the part were at least fifteen years younger than me."

I got the job... so much for being too old. My weather beaten face worked for me that day. They sent me to truck driving school. I got my 18-wheel driver's license and for three years, two weeks a year, I drove that big red semi all over the West. They shot enough footage for three feature films. One time they shot film of me driving their truck all the way from Flagstaff, Arizona, to Page; one hundred thirty-three miles.

The best part was when we worked all day in Monument Valley. That's where "She Wore a Yellow Ribbon," "The Searchers," "Wagonmaster," and other westerns were filmed. John Ford movies had miles and miles of the "out west" in the background. And in the fore-ground, John Wayne, Ward Bond, Harry Carey, Jr., Ben Johnson, Victor Mc Laglen, and two wonderful guys I worked with for three and a half years on "Wagon Train," Terry Wilson and Frank McGrath. They were on one horse. I had four hundred horses under me.

At sunset - at the foot of "The Mittens" – "GHOST RIDERS IN THE SKY"... I got chills all over. I miss those guys.

CHAPTER 46
I LOVE LUCY, TOO

Play Ball! That's what the director said to Lucille Ball. You see we were making a TV commercial for the game "Slam Back"... i.e., one of those games where you bat a tiny ball back and forth by spinning several tiny dowels with a bunch of tiny paddles attached at right angles to the pole. Your opponent does the same from the opposite side of the table. Points are scored when you bat the ball or puck into the goal at the end of the playing board. The goal can be a hole or a net, or both.

Ms. Ball had just worked all day, around twelve hours, on "I Love Lucy." She was tired and a little giddy. You know how you get when you're bushed and know you still have work to do. She flitted around the set until the director, a good friend of hers, yelled, "Someone nail her down and we'll get this done and we can all go home."

We got the shot of the two of us playing the game. She won. She was good and it was also in the script.

They got close-ups of the game being played and the last shot was the two of us, side by side, with Lucy selling the game. I don't remember all her lines but the last thing she says is, "Isn't that right, coach?" At which point she gives me a jab in the ribs with her elbow. Each time we rehearsed the jab got a little harder.

Play ball!

The director asked Lucy if she wanted to shoot it. She said, "Shoot!" And then looked up at me and asked, "Am I hitting you too hard?" I leaned down and whispered in her ear, "If you hear me break wind – you'll know."

Lucy couldn't continue for a while. Why? Laughter got in the way. I was nine feet tall. This "Ball of Fire" that had made millions laugh, millions of times – I got her to laugh once. A small thank you for all the laughs she had given me.

I don't think they sold many games. "Slam Back" is not a household name but Lucy IS, and I know I'll always cherish the evening I played with that Ball.

# CHAPTER 47
BE A CLONE

My dad was a clone. There were two of him, Ben and Len, identical twins. Dad was Ben. I was about five years old when I first saw them standing next to each other. Uncle Len had been working in a South American hospital. He was an M.D.

I immediately started to cry. I couldn't tell which one was Dad. They knelt down right away and tried to explain why all of the sudden I had two fathers. Like Yule Brenner said, "Was a puzzlement!" They were identical. I had to take them at their word, which was which, because they were the only ones there that knew.

Like all twins, they were really close. I watch those twin conventions on TV; hundreds of identical twins gather to study and be studied. Identical twins communicate on levels the rest of us don't have access to. They are beautiful and mysterious to watch. I wish Ben and Len had spent more time together so I could have watched them more. Green Bay General Hospital and UCLA took up their time.

While writing this chapter, I got a call from Judy Yeager of Shelbyville, Indiana. Judy started her call, "You don't know me but I am calling to invite you to a celebration." She explained that the alumni, students, faculty and administrators of Waldron High School were going to honor their 1926-1927 Basketball team. That team had gone to the Indiana State Finals and finished their winning season with a 20-1 record. The "Banner Hanging" ceremony was to happen between the Junior Varsity and Varsity games.

The Miller twins (identical twins), Ben and Len, led the team that season, seventy-eight years ago. I have many fond memories of my dad. Now I can thank the basketball fans of Waldron High School for another.

Only in Indiana can a seventy-eight-year-old memory of nine teenage boys, lead by their first-year coach, Bill Webb, and their winning teamwork on a basketball court (which is now the Fire Department House) jump out of the distant past and grab your heart!

Now here are a few coincidences to ponder... the 2003-2004 Waldron High School Basketball team is led by their first year coach, Jason Delaney. The team won the Indiana State 1A High School Tournament and finished the season with a 27-0 record. They were the only unbeaten team in the state.

Way to go Mohawks!

Waldron High School 1926-27 State Tournament Team

First row (l to r): Roy Yeager and Maurice Clay; Second row (l to r): Len Miller, Louie Neibert, Malcolm Clay, Ralph Lux, and Ben Miller; Second row (l to r): George Cuskaden, Principal Tom Fogarty, Lawrence Craig, Coach Bill Webb, and Norman Kanouse.

Waldron High School 2004 Class 1A State Champions

First row (l to r) Cheerleaders: Tiana Kohler, Meleah Fields, Nicole Anderson, Joni Wettrick, Jessica Phares, and Becky Allen. Second row (l to r): Mike Stamper (Principal), Brian Fehribach (Athletic Director), Bryan Hurst, Justin Sawyer, Jimmy Eikman, Ben Thomas, James Dixon, Brad Kuhn, Kyle Alexander, Kurt Mink, Ralph Lux (Manager), and Ryan Wallace. Third row (l to r): Gary Fralich (Assistant Coach): Brian Asher (Assistant Coach): Jason Lemmons, Justin Barnard, Jordan Barnard, John Vierling (Manager), and Jason Delaney (Head Coach). Not pictured: Somer Case (Manager) and Chelsey Milbourn (Cheerleader).

- 1927 Team had a first year coach — Bill Webb
- 2004 Team had a first year coach — Jason Delaney
- 1927 Team leading scorers were Ben and Len Miller
- 2004 Team leading scorers were Justin and Jordan Barnard — You guessed it... two sets of identical twins!

The basketball-playing clones, with their fellow players are not hard to find in these team photos.

The last time the Mohawks played in a championship game was in 1927. Their 27th win came on March 27, 2004. This time around they are the Champs. Maybe that theory, "six degrees of separation," is for real.

I was a clone too. At one time there were forty of me. Britt Ekland and I had thirty-nine identical twins, each. We lived on a planet made of ice called Ice Station Zebra. "Battlestar Galactica" was our birthplace. I forget the name of the scriptwriter who thought us up.

I had fun walking up to a guy with my face mask on and saying, "If I was you – and I am!" I heard a few nervous giggles from behind the masks.

Hollywood has been in the business of cloning for a long time. A successful show on TV, one with high ratings (a bigger number of people watching them than the other shows in their time slot) will be cloned.

"Wagon Train" is just one of the examples. With its high ratings it got two clones – "Rawhide" and "Bonanza." Each show starred four actors. "Wagon Train" had Ward Bond for the over-fifty audience - the grand father figure; Terry Wilson, the father figure; Robert Horton, the hunk for the ladies out there in TV land; and Frank McGrath, the comedic cook, the comedy relief. "Rawhide" and "Bonanza" were cooked up using the same recipe, the same formula. Four guys, the same age groups. "Rawhide" and "Wagon Train" each had a cook, both with beards, both identical size and their names started with the same letter, Wooster and Wishbone.

They were different shows in one way. "Wagon Train" moved people from east to west. "Rawhide" moved cattle from south to north and, in "Bonanza," people just passed through.

Rowdy, on "Rawhide," was to become one of the most talented actors, directors and producers in film history. Clint Eastwood's three careers are second to none. He even writes the musical scores for his films.

Clint doesn't need me to defend him in any way, but I get angry when I hear someone, anyone, call him anything but a great actor. Don Rickles, in fun, said, "I just came from a Clint Eastwood film... I watched a fly fall asleep on his lower lip!"

I know Don Rickles makes a living ribbing everybody. I don't know how many people, including actors, know that one of the toughest things for an actor to do on film is NOTHING! When a director says "Action," it takes great courage and confidence for an actor to do nothing.

Most accomplished film actors allow the audience to participate in the telling of the story. They don't chew up the scenery. They allow the imagination of the audience access. "Come on in. This is not much different from reading a book. Fill in the pause – get mad or sad or glad with me." Strong personalities can do that. Nothing.

It doesn't hurt to look like Eastwood or Wayne or Bond or Bogart or Fonda or Pitt or Redford. When you look like that and you have the confidence, the guts, you can let the audience help you tell the story.

As soon as Clint formed his own production company, he could wear three hats while making a film: the hat of a producer, director and star. With all that power, he has never cloned a picture. I hope he works forever.

If not cloning, Hollywood produces sequels, series, and remakes. Sequels like "Death Wish I, II, III" or "Lethal Weapon I, II, III and IV." The thinking is, if "I" made money, so will "II" and "III" etc. Series like "Star Trek The Beginning," then "Star Trek The Middle," and "Star Trek Almost The End," and "Star Trek The End," and "Star Trek The New Beginning," can last years; they are big moneymakers.

"Tarzan The Ape Man," starring Johnny Weissmuller, in 1932 was the original. Then came the remakes. Twenty-seven years later, in 1959, "Tarzan The Ape Man," the same story, different "monkey" man, and twenty-two years pass, and Bo Derek produces the same story, "Tarzan The Ape Man." Remakes seldom improve the film. These films got worse with each telling. The last two lost money.

The most successful method of filmmaking is to re-issue, rerun old film. Disney has brought back their animated classics every six or seven years. They bring out their big hits: "Dumbo," "Fantasia," "Pinochio," "Snow White," "Sleeping Beauty." They make a bundle and their audience is delighted. Why? Every seven years there's a new set of little fannies in those seats.

Money, money, money, money... that's what cloning, sequels, series, remakes and reruns mean. Hollywood is a business, an entertainment business.

The Latin inscription that wraps around the MGM Lion reads, ARS GRATIA ARTIS – Art For The Sake Of Art... RIGHT!

Front: Frank McGrath and "Scott" Miller.
Back: Terry Wilson and John McIntyre.

CHAPTER 48
A ROBOT AND A RABBIT

Turtles and unicorns... Cortney, my daughter, slept inside a unicorn for the first two years of her life. A turtle and a giraffe were riding a merry-go-round so close by she could touch them.

This magical bedroom came from the marvelous mind of Dick Gautier. It came as no surprise to me. Dick can do anything and has done everything. As an actor he played "Jamie The Robot" on the TV series "Get Smart." You couldn't name a TV show during the past forty years that he hadn't guest-starred on.

On Broadway, he played the lead role of Conrad in the very successful musical, "Bye Bye Birdie." Paul Lynde, Dick Van Dyke and Chita Rivera played along with him.

He's written books on cartooning, "How to Draw Caricatures," books on "Actors as Artists," and "Musicians as Artists." He paints with whimsy in his brush. Whenever he draws, sings, dances, does stand-up comedy, he amuses... and, he is a friend to children of all ages.

He also made unicorns out of little girls' cribs. He put a huge carved woodenhead at one end of the crib and a three-inch thick tail at the other. The head had big costume jewelry eyes and a little wooden horn. The reins were of shiny beads and the tail and head were painted bright yellow with a red mane. What a way to go to dreamland!

He carved the merry-go-round with a turtle, a giraffe and a pig. Then he glued it on the six-foot by six-foot mirror on the wall beside the unicorn. When Cortney looked at it, she saw herself riding her unicorn right along with the turtle and his friends. It was a magical ride to start out her life.

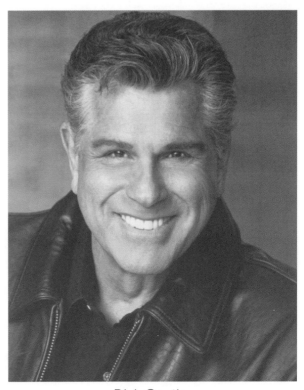

Dick Gautier.

Cortney Miller.

"Imagination is more important than information," said Albert Einstein. Dick Gautier has known that for a long time. Check out his website for more visions of his imagination. www.DickGautier.com.

Cortney recently got married. She and Bill Hannan, her husband, asked me to perform the wedding service. In Santa Barbara County, if you don't have a police record, you can get a permit to do that. So, I did.

I didn't own a suit. I don't need one for my lifestyle. But I needed one for the wedding. It wouldn't do to have presided at such an important occasion in casual clothes. I do not believe that clothes make the man, but Cortney has helped make me a man.

I had a drinking problem years ago. I wouldn't stop or couldn't stop. I never drank when I worked, but between jobs I did. And there were a lot of "in betweens." My drinking was beginning to get in the way of my life.

Then Cortney happened. She saved my life. Up until her birth I wouldn't stop drinking for anybody, including me. She made my life worthwhile. She helped me get real.

I'm reminded of the lines in Margery Williams' beautiful poem, "The Velveteen Rabbit,"

"Real isn't how you are made, said the Skin Horse.
"It's a thing that happens to you.
When a child loves you for a long, long time,
Not just to play with,
But Really Loves You, then you become REAL."

"That was a great many years ago;
but once you are Real
you can't become unreal again.
It lasts for always."

Thank you, Cortney.
Love,
Dad

Dream on, Cortney.

CHAPTER 49
THE SINGING CURATOR

Have you ever seen a book walking? I have. Well it was more like a whole library. This man soaks up information, all kinds of information and files it in his noggin. He carries it (it's not heavy, it's his druther) for you and me.

We can have a piece of his mind anytime, anywhere, just for the asking. He'll dish it out on paper because he knows a short pencil is better than a long memory.

He wraps his thoughts with humor and wit, making even dull subjects bright and colorful. Like Charles Russell, he is a "Word Painter."

He had a long and successful singing career. He warbled for years in the footlights at Radio City Music Hall in New York. The volume and projection of his voice is still heard each time he starts off a Dum-Dum with a glass-breaking Tarzan yell.

But now his voice is carried by literary means. His songs have become music to the eyes. His lyrics, written by Edgar Rice Burroughs, are enjoyed by faithful fans that wait, four times a year, to see his production called the *Burroughs Bulletin*. This hit show has had a fifty-seven year run.

Critics and fans praise it as the best fanzine ever. For seventeen years, it has been his paper opera, his song. This walking fountain of words I've been talking about is George T. McWhorter. He is the Editor and Publisher of the *Burroughs Bulletin*. He is also Curator of the Burroughs Memorial Collection, University of Louisville Library, University of Louisville, Louisville, Kentucky.

Robert Grudin, author of the book, "Time and The Art of Living," wrote "Speak of literary art as teaching, delighting, celebrating, communicating, preserving, convincing. But speak of it also as gift-giving, the shy gift-giving of intensely sociable people."

Thank you, George, for sharing your gifts.

George T. McWhorter in his "native" environment.

Cortney and Bill Hannon and the "Old Man of the Cloth."

CHAPTER 50
FROM BLACK AND WHITE TO COLOR

Weddings make me nervous. I've only attended four. I managed to make it through my own without falling down. I was "best man" at two. Even that label made me feel uneasy. It's a misnomer. If I'm the best man there, does that make my best friend second best man? I don't think so.

The fourth wedding was different. If you go to the Santa Barbara County Court House and pay a fee of fifty dollars and sign a document, they appoint you "Commissioner of Civil Marriages," and you can legally perform the role of Preacher for any marriage.

My daughter Cortney and her fiancée, Bill Hannan, had asked me if I would perform their ceremony. They had found out about this possibility and I leaped at the chance.

They had also written their own service. They put their hearts, their feelings for each other in it - making it their own wedding in a very personal way. It was a pleasure for me to present their thoughts to a congregation of their friends.

First thing I had to do was buy a suit. I hadn't had one for thirty-eight years. Cortney had planned on me wearing a tux, but I pleaded with her to change her mind. I'd like to tweak the person that invented the tux. "Bash" would be a more appropriate word and action.

At most of the important rituals of our lives, the men in our society are expected to attend in black and white, colorless outfits that are a torture to put on and to wear. We are turned into a herd of fidgeting penguin clones trying to keep everything in place and trying even harder not to dip our cuffs in the soup.

All the while, the women are dressed in every color of the spectrum; so proud of their originality and beauty that they will kill the woman who shows up in the same dress. What a concept! Try and find another species on earth that the male allows that.

I walked Cortney down the aisle. That's not what happened. She walked me down the aisle. She was composed, relaxed, in charge. Bill and I were bundles of raw nerves.

I presented her to Bill, took a step around them and turned to face them and the congregation. The first thing that happened...Cortney straightened Bill's bow tie. That didn't surprise me. Bill was wearing a TUX. It was too late to warn him.

CHAPTER 51
WRITE ON

He can get people to laugh. That's a talent I wish more people possessed.

After working on eleven TV sit-coms as an assistant writer, he can look back on all those scripts he was involved with and see that he contributed more jokes than a lot of the other writers.

He wrote an episode of "Sister, Sister" in four days. It sold and has aired four or five times. That's more than a large percent of the writers in the history of TV have sold.

He also wrote four other sit-com scripts on spec. They were all funny, very funny. And yet it has taken him ten years to write those four scripts. Writing scripts for movies or TV is hard work. If you're a perfectionist like Brad, it's very hard work. I think making a career in Hollywood as a writer is tougher than making it as an actor, a dancer, a singer, a director, a cameraman... you name it, writing is tougher.

Because Brad has this gift of seeing the world as a funny place, full of funny people, he has become a successful disc jockey. He helps people to break out of their shells at parties and graduations and all kinds of get-togethers. With his help, they start to have fun in spite of themselves. He breaks the ice, warms up the place. "I saw a man, he danced with his wife and it wasn't in Chicago" – it was Brad.

He's still writing. I hope he keeps on writing. He's a very good writer. He is also my son.

Like father, like son... both UCLA grads.

Brad Miller.

# CHAPTER 52
CRITICS

The movies and TV shows I like to watch are comedies. They are becoming an endangered species. War is not fun entertainment. Blood and body parts are for the true grit crowd. I agree with people that say violent films can teach us that violence is so painful, so ugly that no one in his right mind would want to go there. But I already know that. Took me a long time, but now that violence is not a part of my amusement package, I plan to stay on that diet the rest of my life.

Feel-good films, TV shows and plays are important to my well-being. They make me feel healthy. Norman Cousins called laughter, "inner aerobics." I'll buy that. Give me a giggle, guffaw – chuckle or chortle – and I'll pay gladly for the ticket.

The two reasons I search for that "make me cry" are: one, because I'm laughing so hard I can't stop, and the second reason is when I experience beauty... so much beauty that my whole being is filled with it - the beauty of a sunset or sunrise, the beauty of a kind gesture... the beauty of a glorious view of Mother Nature. Like the view the young cavalry lieutenant saw when he discovered Yosemite Valley. He burst into tears, overwhelmed by so much beauty.

These are the things I look for in a film. Now there's a group of people called CRITICS. I'm sure most of them are nice

> **"Critics should be treated like the king and queen's food tasters. Don't pay any attention to them until one of them drops dead after sampling a performance."**

folks. It's their job to get between you and a film, and tell you what you're going to see before you see it. A lot of them get wrapped in the process. Some compete with other critics to see who can sound the most witty, informed and knowledgeable about how to make movies. Sadly, according to most of them, the movie they have just seen hasn't been made up to their standards.

There have been lots of bad movies made and more stinkers will be made. But critics paint an awful picture about most pictures.

There have been good critics. Charles Champlin was one for over twenty-five years for the *Los Angeles Times*. His column of criticism usually went like this, "These are *my* thoughts about this film. Go see it and see what you think." Constructive criticism, not destructive.

TV film critics are my favorite. I have one in mind whose TV personality comes across like that of a not-so-friendly Casper the Friendly Ghost. Only he wears tweeds. His shirt collar is two inches too big for his pencil neck. His tweedy sport coat shoulders are three inches too big for his bony frame, and his voice is so meek, I have to turn up my hearing aid to hear him.

Out of this mousy creature comes a verbal attack on most of the movies he's seen kinda like that of a crazed giant with a machete in both hands and a bottle of poison between his tobacco-stained teeth. He's a mean critter with a poop-eating grin on his face. He absolutely loves his job.

The irony on top of irony is that he's the film critic for *The Wall Street Journal*. That's kinda like being a sportswriter for *Vogue*.

Here's a suggestion. Turn him off. Or watch him for a few laughs and then go see the film and make up your own mind.

I don't know who said this, but somebody did. Our responsibility when looking at a work of art, whether it's a film, painting, play, dance or sculpture - is not to UNDERstand it, but just to be able to STAND it.

Critics should be treated like the king's and queen's food tasters. Don't pay any attention to them until one of them drops dead after sampling a performance.

In 1964, David Moss was a toreador in Spain.

CHAPTER 53
TOREADOR-AGENT-FRIEND

Hollywood agents can make or break an actor's career. They're that important. I don't know any working actor, in film or TV, who doesn't have one.

My first agent, Robert Raison, was totally responsible for starting my career. I would have been a basketball coach all my professional life if he hadn't given me his card that day in the fifties. I believe in "happy accidents". That was one.

I've always envied actors who have an agent that is also their friend. Tom Selleck is one. There are many others. They are very lucky actors.

There is an old saying in Hollywood about agents: "Changing agents is like changing deck chairs on the Titanic." Like any old saying, many times it's not true.

Actors get old. Happily, in my case, my gray beard and wrinkles are working for me. Gray hair or no hair, weather-beaten faces, weight gain or loss, beards and limps, new teeth and glasses happen. If an actor still wants to work as this aging process happens, his agent submits him for older roles.

A thing called timing is involved. The agent who represented you in your youth tried to cast you in totally different roles from the roles you are right for years later. It's unfair to blame your agent for not getting you parts at any phase of your career. You're changing, the parts available are changing, the casting directors are being changed, and the viewing public's tastes are changing.

Examples - Blond, blue eyed, scar-faced men were in demand as the bad guys when we were at war with Germany, the same with Oriental actors when Japan was our enemy. Cowboy types made good careers when there were twenty-six Western TV shows on per week. There's not one Western TV series on now, unless you count reruns.

Is it a mystery that very few actors have film careers that last ten years? The most asked question in show biz: "Whatever happened to what's his name?"

So an agent who is also your friend — is a gift. When you're turned down for an acting job, it's a one hundred percent rejection. You weren't turned down for a bad sales pitch for the car you're trying to sell. You didn't get the part because they didn't like the fit of the shoes you peddle. You didn't get the job because they didn't think YOU fit the part. If you can't deal with that much rejection, get out of town. Actors at ALL levels of success have to deal with pure rejection. It ain't easy, but most of them are dreamers and it takes a lot to kill a dream.

Here's where an agent who is your friend enters the picture. Friendship doesn't happen overnight. Good friends get through all your baggage layer by layer and still stick around. It takes time. And when rejection strikes, a friendly agent gives you support.

When I got sick and incapable of holding my job, David was there. His frequent phone calls propped me up when I needed propping.

When I had regained my health, David called one day and said, "Now that you're feeling good, why don't I call your old boss and see if he's interested in working with you again?" The thought hadn't entered my mind and I told him so. "You mind if I give him a call?" David asked.

"I think that'd really be a long shot." I mumbled. Not working for so long left me with a short supply of self-confidence.

"I'll call him," he said.

Two weeks later I was on a plane to New York. The screen test went well. Well, I guess it did because I'm back at my old job now. Been back for three years. My whole life has been turned around. Why? Because David Moss is my agent and he is also my good friend.

I forgot to mention, David made a living in his youth as a toreador. No bull. In Spain, when he was a young man, he fought bulls in the ring. He faced death every Sunday. He almost bought it twice when he was gored. Today, at sixty something, he still fights bulls three times a year in northern Mexico. I'm pretty sure he's the only agent in the history of agents that fights that kind of bull. So he's not only my good friend and my agent, he's a fearless S.O.B. That fearless part comes in handy in Hollywood.

My agent, David Moss.

David Moss, toreador at age 69.

CHAPTER 54
SNAP OUT OF IT!

Art Buchwald, former First Lady Barbara Bush, Mike Wallace, Mariette Hartley, Sally Field, Marial Hemmingway, Dick Cavett and I were mentally ill. I mean it. Winston Churchill was one of us. John Lynch, safety for the Tampa Buccaneers, in his twenties, has got it. Millions of Americans are sick in the head.

It's an invisible disease. Dis–ease. Like diabetes, you can't tell by looking who has it. A psychiatrist can tell. You can't hide from them. You will probably try to hide the disease because of the confusion that goes with having it, but a good shrink will find it.

If you are suffering from a feeling of hopelessness, weight loss, totally screwed up sleep cycles, a deep sense of worthlessness, an inability to concentrate, fear (of anything and everything), a complete absence of joy in your life, and you haven't got a clue why you feel that way – you've got it.

It's called "Clinical Depression." It's caused by a chemical imbalance in your brain. You need help. Three out of ten people who have this disease commit suicide. Get help. See a psychiatrist fast.

There are over twenty drugs that are used to bring credibility back into your life. I take four each day.

For some people, one prescription will do the trick. Everyone reacts differently to the different drugs. I had to take eight drugs, one at a time, for periods of eight weeks before the doctor found a combination that would work for me. You also have to wait at least two weeks before starting on a new drug. The trials took about two years before we found the recipe that kicked in for me.

"Sad, depressed?" "You don't have anything in your life to be depressed about!" That's the reaction you'll get from friends and family. They can't understand how badly you feel. Sally Field said she only got out of bed to go to the bathroom for two years. Two years! And she had two little children at the time.

Dick Cavett said at one time he was so depressed, so tired, so full of fear and despair he was unable to do anything. Even if he saw the thing or person he desired more than anything in the world, just three steps across the room, he couldn't, wouldn't go get it.

The psychiatrist I go to for check-ups has a pillow with the picture of a guy knitted on it.

One of his patients with clinical depression gave it to him. The guy is yelling, "SNAP OUT OF IT!" The doctor sits on it in his office.

You bet there is a stigma that goes with this package. Tell your boss you're out of your head, you're mentally ill, you have a sick mind, and you have a chemical imbalance and see how fast you're unemployed. But with a doctor's care and the new anti-depressant drugs, we can live joyful, productive lives. I've been there – done that.

I had been a spokesman for Gorton's for ten years and had another year to go on my contract. Before my doctor could find the effective prescription for me, I was too tired, too fearful, so unsure of myself that I called my boss and told him I was too sick to do competent work. He released me from my contract. It was the saddest day of my life. I felt totally worthless.

Two years later with my doctor's care and the right prescription, I was alive again. That may sound phony but let me tell you, it is not. That's how good it feels. I got my old job back, too.

I'm certainly not the only one who has received help. More and more people with the disease have been helped back to health. People like Rosalynn Carter, the former First Lady, and Dr. Kay Jamison are on a mission to educate us about the disease. And they are getting results.

John Lynch came back. He almost lost his job as an outstanding safety on the Super Bowl-winning Tampa Bay Buccaneers. But with the support of his coach, John Grudin, Lynch's wife and family, a few of his teammates and a good doctor, he's playing pro football for one of the best teams in the world. His toughest opponent in his young life has been Clinical Depression and he beat it. You can, too.

> **"Three out of ten people who have this disease commit suicide. Get help. See a psychiatrist fast."**

Winston Churchill called it, "The big black dog that sleeps at my feet." He managed to become one of the world's most successful leaders and he accomplished that without the aid of anti-depressant drugs.

But you and I, with professional medical help and the use of these wonderful new drugs can be the best humans we can be. They have saved my life. I will take them as long as my doctor tells me.

Go get it... HELP. It's out there. GET IT!

CHAPTER 55
A TENTION

Some people thrive on attention. They seem never to get enough. They start early in their lives.

"Hey, Mom – Dad watch me dive in the lake!"

"Look Mom, I ate all my carrots!"

"Mom, Dad – all of you guests. This time I'll play for you Bach's C Major in Minor!"

"Teacher, Johnny gave you the wrong answer. The right answer is..."

"For my seventh song I'll sing... And then there was the one about two sailors and a monkey."

And on their gravestone - "See, I told you I was sick!"

Attention is food for these people. Others get so much attention it becomes A—tension. If they don't find a quiet harbor, an escape, a place to be alone, attention becomes a poison.

"I vant to be alone!" said Greta Garbo, one of the most beautiful, talented, successful actresses in the world. She ended up being alone. Some say, to save her life, her sanity.

James Arness, the star of the most successful TV series ever, had a public relations man whose job was to keep him and his name and his family out of the news. Since his retirement he has disappeared. He protected and cherished his privacy.

Johnny Carson, after twenty years, five nights a week of going to bed with millions across the country has vanished. He's had enough attention and has chosen a life out of the limelight.

It's hard to imagine that people can make a living on stage and then be content to spend the rest of their lives in the audience. It happens.

Those folks who ignore or aren't aware of a need for a healthy dose of quiet now and then sometimes crash and burn. Elvis Presley comes to mind. There have been many others who couldn't deal with fame. They opted to take their life quickly or slow and painfully, like Elvis. Too much attention turned into A tension. If you can't handle it, too much adoration, too much love from too many people can kill you.

Meanwhile those other creatures among us that you can never turn off – that can never turn themselves off will keep on keeping on.

"And for my next number..."

"Have you heard the one about the fish that..."

"My mother taught me this step when I was three."

"And here's a picture when I was in the junior high marching band!"

"I'll make a doggie out of the red balloon."

You and I will have to learn to tell them, "I vant to be alone!" It's for our own good.

Besides, like the comic Brother Dave Gardner said, "If we ever find out what we're doing, we'll probably go hide!"

Nancy, my life saver!

CHAPTER 56
LOVE CONQUERS ALL

"Tempus fugit." Time flies, said the Greeks.

Not always. Not when you're depressed. Time stretches out like a long, upward, unending trail as dark as the inside of a statue's head, when you are depressed.

I don't mean sad. Sad is when you lose a dollar. Sad is when you drop your ice cream cone. Sad is a minor feeling.

Try to imagine losing your best friend, and your job, and being told you have cancer, and that your house burned to the ground and that you are going to have all your teeth pulled. You will still be in a state of sad compared to being depressed. Multiply that feeling of sadness by a million times, and you'll still feel much better than you would if you felt depressed. I hope you never have to go there. It's just a few steps this side of being dead.

Everyone needs help if they get depressed. It's an invisible disease. Not many people understand it. They find it hard to believe you're sick. You do, too.

Some people never get better. Three out of ten commit suicide. I was on the edge many times.

A doctor I trusted, the anti-depressants he prescribed, and the love and support of a woman saved my life. Nancy gave me the love and courage to struggle through the gloom, waiting for the drugs to take effect.

It took two years. I've been back among the living for more than three years. When I compare those periods of time, my memory distorts them. Being depressed for two years seems like a century. Being healthy these past few years seems like a day. Time flies when you are healthy.

One of my favorite books is "Time and The Art of Living" by Robert Grudin. In a chapter on memory he writes, "If we really love health and hate disease, we should study and remember our illnesses, because the memory of disease makes mere health a luxurious pleasure."

Nancy and Dr. Ronald Pollack, along with my agent, David Moss, and the Gorton's company have given me not only the luxury of good health, but also the awareness to cherish it. Am I indebted to them... what do you think?!

CHAPTER 57
FROM CHIMP TO SHRIMP

We could make out the New England coast through the porthole. Gloucester was off our port bow. The seas were calm but the boat has a steady roll, a consistent rock. Not a coffee cup-grabbing roll but a "feet-wide-apart when you're walking the deck" roll.

I was at the helm. I'd just been given a higher rank and felt proud to have the responsibility.

The director yelled "Cut, take five." I stepped off the rocking set and walked right into the make-up man. I was the new GORTON'S FISHERMAN, and I was seasick. Maybe not seasick, just a little bit dizzy. After all, we were filming on a sound stage in the middle of Manhattan.

It wouldn't do to have a sea captain suffering from mal de mer in the middle of New York City, on dry land. Gorton's future TV commercial shoots would be done at sea.

No one seemed to notice. No one offered me pills or a bucket, not even an ice pack. My spokesman job was safe, at least for the moment.

They never asked me at the audition if I was a good sailor. It slipped my mind to mention that I got seasick on a car-ferry on Lake Michigan, a half an hour out of Chicago.

I had tried Dramamine on the troop ship coming back from duty in Germany. It knocked me out. I was in a deep sleep in half an hour. That wouldn't help when it came to dialogue.

Two Marezine pills and I could sail through a hurricane on a cork and not get seasick and not nod off. I had just forgotten to take them. Well, that's not quite true. I didn't think a gently rocking set would get to me. Surprise!

> **"It slipped my mind to mention that I got seasick on a car-ferry on Lake Michigan, a half an hour out of Chicago."**

Since my Manhattan Project, we've done over fifty commercials, some in Tampa Bay in forty-knot winds. Darn – I forgot to mention the boat was tied to the wharf. We worked in the Straights of Juan De Fucha out of Vancouver, B.C. Marezine was there. We went out of San Pedro Harbor, Los Angeles... no problem.

After fifteen years you could call me an old salt. Well maybe just old.

There was only one hitch. Around my seventh year, Gorton's was purchased from General Mills, by Unilever. It was a hostile takeover, at least as far as I was concerned. Unilever owned a fish company in Europe, and they had been using a European actor for their TV spots. So it was bye-bye for me.

Most actors love to act, whether it's on the live stage (legitimate) or the TV and film stage (illegitimate). It's the time between jobs that is tough. I had teaching to fall back on, and did need its support financially and psychologically, many times. Some actors get lost in their down time. Many just throw in the towel.

When I lost the Gorton's contract, I taught school. Six months after my release, Gorton's called my agent and asked if I'd be interested in having my old job back. Does a sea captain need Marezine? Where do I sign?

It seems that when Gorton's tested the European fisherman's television spots, the results were less than positive. I was told he played a jolly "Pied Piper of Hamlin" character; a roly-poly guy with lots of children dancing along the wharf with him. The spots didn't go over big with the mothers out in TV land.

So I got a new supply of Marezine. Several years back, Gorton's was bought from Unilever by a Japanese company. This time it was a friendly take-over and the good friends in Gloucester, Massachusetts (Gorton's headquarters) kept me along for the ride.

I hope the job goes on and on. It's a very good company to work for. I have made many friends there.

Fish is good for you and me. Gorton's sells twice as much fish as their nearest competitor. The Gorton's Fisherman has been catching fish for over 150 years and he knows all the best places to fish. TRUST HIM!

CHAPTER 58
GRANDMOTHER'S CRAFETERIA

"Not that phone book! Please use the other... See, I told you."

Whoops! The floor was scattered with what, at first glance, looked like dried bugs of some sort. The small odd shaped things turned out to be dried flowers, tiny Lupin blossoms. Leaves of different shapes and color and all colors of flowers.

Mom had been pressing them in the phone book. I know better now. Never pick up a book, especially a large book, in her house. It may be the temporary home for hundreds of flowers.

She uses them to decorate fragile, beautiful greeting cards. She can turn a flattened Lupin blossom into a hovering hummingbird. Another flower will change into a miniature palm tree. These creations hang, drying in rows, suspended on twine that crisscrosses the rooms of her home. It becomes a challenge to walk through these rooms without being captured in a web of fluttering, transparent, card-sized flower arrangements.

> **"...she has grown over five hundred tomatoes in one season. We think she sings to them. She must have a 'green hum.'"**

On the one-foot wide, forty-foot long piece of land peeking out between huge slabs of thick cement between her mobile home and the next one, she has grown over five hundred tomatoes in one season. We think she sings to them. She must have a "green hum." She can grow flowers and vegetables where even weeds fear to bed.

You know those fat books of fabric swatches that designers show you to pick out the material to make your custom curtains or cover your couch? The cloth comes in many sizes, from 6x8 inches to 2x2 feet.

A local decorator retired, and Mom inherited a closet full of these foot-thick collections of colorful cloth. Several years later they were gone. In their place had been a parade of stuffed clowns, Raggedy Ann dolls, jewelry bags, tea cozies, potholders and padded gloves, bunnies with enormous ears (a different color than their plump bodies), dolls for every holiday, laundry bags... The parade marched to the Methodist Church, all the grandchildren and some of the children (I saw to it I got my share), and neighbors and their kids and their kids' kids.

All that joy from a pile of stuff that would have been trashed if she hadn't been so crafty.

The kitchen calls and mom answers with cakes and pies and buns and bread and cookies and candy that would make Willie Wonka proud.

Stews and roasts and soups and baked chickens and turkeys and hams are there. She can make meals for two or twenty. I recommend it all. Maybe I'd go a little light on the carrot soup. But all the rest is making me drool right now.

In her spare time, she is the family historian. She writes more letters than President Thomas Jefferson. She knows the family tree including that part that's underground.

Mom is color-coordinated at all times. Whether she makes the clothes she's wearing or she buys them from some catalogue, they will match. The shoes with the skirt, the blouse with the scarf, and the jewelry with all... in vogue, in style, up to date, sharp.

She's seen the whole world. Dad and she went to all the Olympics during Dad's sabbaticals.

Mom and her three men.

She has a necklace or two from every country. She has ten million color slides of their travels. She'll show them to anyone she cares about, and she cares about everyone.

For fun, she devours murder mysteries. She reads one a day, sometimes two, if the glue hasn't dried on her greeting cards. Her son, Kent, keeps her supplied by buying used books at thrift shops. She's read every mystery in all the local libraries.

> **"The kitchen calls and mom answers with cakes and pies and buns and bread and cookies and candy that would make Willie Wonka proud."**

She eats more ice-cream than any three people. Vanilla is her favorite, but if you don't have it, ANY other flavor will do.

TV is a treat. She's seen every episode of "Murder She Wrote" four times. Her favorite show right now is "Monk." She recommended it to the rest of the family and now we're all hung up on it. It's a murder mystery, what else?

I'd say Mom has had and is still having a full life. With all her varied interests and hobbies and loves, it's still a quiet life. You see, Mom has been deaf for two decades. But I think, the whole family thinks, everyone who knows her thinks she hears the song of life as well as anybody. At ninety-two, it's been a long song.

CHAPTER 59
DOWN THE ROAD A PEACE

"ROAD WORK AHEAD." In the summer of 2003, I drove 5,000 miles from Las Vegas to Louisville, Kentucky, then north to Chicago and back to Vegas through Iowa, Nebraska, Colorado, New Mexico and Arizona.

I saw Bloomington, Indiana, where my folks met at school, Indiana University. I hadn't been back there since I was in fourth grade. The town had changed just a little. I was born there in 1934 and in just seventy years, there had been some ROAD WORK BEHIND.

It took me twenty-four days to drive through all those places. I stopped in Louisville for five days to attend a Tarzan fan convention. I stayed in Chicago for five days to work at the AARP convention for Gorton's. And Denver grabbed me for two days with good food and interesting museums. So, with those stops I'd really traveled five thousand miles in around thirteen days. Easy days. Collecting beautiful vistas and people all the way.

Back home in Vegas, after answering four hundred fifty e-mails, I sat down with a cup of coffee and took a look in my travel bag of memories. Here are some of the things I found... a field of sunflowers swaying in the breeze in Iowa... a lazy tour up and down the Chicago River in the cool shadow of the architectural forest along its banks. It's the only river that changed its direction. I mean it had its direction changed. It used to flow into Lake Michigan, but now man has made it flow out.

I remember a man high in the mountains of Colorado. He stopped us for ten minutes to wait for a pilot truck to lead us over a section of road being repaired. His road that day was three feet long.

He would stand facing on-coming traffic with his sign reading STOP and then when the pilot truck arrived and turned around he would step back and change his sign to SLOW.

The pilot truck arrived and the driver pulled over and stopped. He turned off the engine, got out and disappeared into the woods.

The sign man said, "It'll be just a few minutes." Just enough time to memorize the snow-covered peaks around us.

An electrical storm in Nebraska came out of my travel bag next and frightened me for the second time. Bolts of lightning cracked the sky into black chunks. Five, ten, so many at once we couldn't count them. Every car and truck headed for cover. Ours was called Holiday Inn.

I remembered a gray-haired lady (there were many) at the AARP convention pulling at the sleeve of my Gorton's fisherman slicker.

> "When I leaned down to hear her better she whispered, 'I remember you — I'm old.'"

When I leaned down to hear her better she whispered, "I remember you — I'm old."

I took a sip of coffee and looked out the window at our back yard. I smiled, remembering Hal, a basketball coach from Indiana, shaking my hand at the Tarzan convention and saying "My Dad played basketball against your dad in high school, in 1929." Hoosiers love basketball and the kids and men that play it.

Mountains and valleys and forests and streams of Colorado spilled out of my travel bag. Some so beautiful they brought tears. I taught at Fort Lewis College in Colorado one summer. The campus was there in my bag, along with the toot of the toy tourist train that goes from Durango through the mountains to Silverton everyday during the summer.

I could see the face of our waitress at the "Country Kitchen" in Flagstaff, Arizona. She was a student at the U. of A. You could tell by the way she moved that she believed the food she was serving was the best, and that if it wasn't, she'd see to it that it was.

Deeper in my bag I found a note. It was written on a used crumpled empty envelope. It had been pinned under the windshield wiper of my car. I found it there when I came out of a diner after having lunch. It read: "Have a nice day – and watch out for that tree." Signed, Plymouth Indiana. My Nevada license reads – XTARZAN.

Just before Nancy and I got home – just south of Boulder Dam, we drove by a huge electrical warning sign. It read – EXPECT DELAYS – 2003 TO 2007.

"ROAD WORK AHEAD." That really means things are improving just around the bend. Just south of where we live, they're going to be improving for the next four years. Keep that thought in your bag.

CHAPTER 60
FATHER KNEW BEST

A sound mind in a sound body. Or in today's language, "An Affirm Mind in a Firm Body". Both describe the Golden Age of Greece. That was my Dad's goal. He wanted to see that Golden Age happen in the U.S. He thought the way to accomplish that was through education – in schools and with the parents.

To reach his goal, he worked very hard to achieve positions of authority where he could influence teachers, administrators, politicians - including presidents and community leaders; people of power who could change policy and educational curricula.

I think he reached those authoritative posts. You tell me. He was Chairman of the Department of Physical Education at UCLA for over ten years. He served on Presidents Eisenhower's and Kennedy's Advisory Committee on Youth Fitness. He was President of the American Academy of Physical Education. He became a charter member and trustee of the American College of Sports Medicine and a Fellow of the American School Health Association and of the American Public Health Association. Remember this is the work of just one man.

He was President of the American Association for Health, Physical Education and Recreation. His career in national and international organizations allowed him many opportunities to travel. He visited over eighty countries and was able to gather information about the history of physical education and sport. He created a class on the subject, which he taught at UCLA. He also organized and was a charter member of the North American Society of Sports Historians.

Dad gave over two hundred fifty addresses in the U.S. and abroad, fifty of which were published. He and Mom attended all the Olympic Games from 1932 to 1984.

I almost forgot: He wrote a book, "PHYSICAL FITNESS FOR BOYS," in 1943 and dedicated it to "The Physical Fitness Leaders of American Youth."

Bragging about my dad? – you bet! Proud? – very! Sad? – terribly!

After over half a century of dedication and hard work, Dad looked at his legacy and this is what he saw.

- The United States has the fattest population in the world.
- The youth of our nation are further from being physically fit than ever.
- Those same youths are starting to have diabetes.

Dad at the White House with President Kennedy.

• Our country is in the midst of an obesity epidemic. The definition of obesity is: "Anyone that is one hundred pounds or more over their healthy weight".

When Dad headed the physical education department (now called the Physiological Science Department) at UCLA, they had over one hundred professors, associate professors, assistants and clerical workers. It now numbers less than twenty people. And, physical education classes are not a requirement for the general student body.

How sad for our country. How sad for Dad. Before he passed on, he saw a society that could be called, "The Golden Age of Grease." He said when a future Darwin chronicles our time here on earth he'll name it, "Survival of the Fattest."

The information on the few pages that follow entitled "TOXIC WAIST," is a condensation of the knowledge about fitness that is available to us all. This knowledge is backed by hundreds of studies made by physical educators, medical doctors, physical therapists and nutritionists who are not selling anything but fitness. These people are not in anybody's pocket. They are independent researchers.

> "Before he passed on, he saw a society that could be called, 'The Golden Age of Grease.'"

Fitness is no big mystery. It's not hard to understand how to be fit. My Dad tried his best to yell it from the rooftops. I've tried to follow his advice and at seventy I know being fit has made my life more enjoyable, more productive and more rewarding. I'm sure Dad would want me to pass the word along.

Thanks Dad! I'm glad I listened. You were right. You still are.

CHAPTER 61
TOXIC WAIST

*Even our best friends won't tell us
"Pssst – you have bad breadth!"*

Our nation stopped expanding after the last wagon train rolled west. But as individuals, we are still rolling on. We are still stretching our boundaries. We and our sons and daughters and our grandchildren are fatter than ever. A recent survey by the National Center for Health Statistics shows that one in five children in the U.S. between the ages of six and seventeen is overweight, and the number is growing. Other studies have shown that if a child is overweight as a teenager, chances are that the person will be overweight as an adult.

The more mature generations are not to be left out in this "larding of our lads and lasses." We are who they look up to – their role models. According to the Mayo Clinic, fifty-five percent of U.S. adults are overweight; that is, over one hundred million overweight role models. When a future Darwin chronicles our lives, the book may be titled "Survival of the Fattest."

Before you tell me overweight people are happier – Santa Claus types – listen to this. Many health care professionals think the worst result of being overweight is psychological stress that comes with the package. It may be unfair and unrealistic, but in our society today, visible fat is a sign of being weak-willed, out-of-control and self-indulgent. Being fat is a big disadvantage in our society because it does not fit with our standards of beauty and sexual attractiveness. That is why we are spending over thirty-three billion dollars a year on diets, weight loss pills, liposuction, fat farms and low cal stuff.

We pay another high price as our excess weight increases. Included in the "battle of the bulge" are health risks to which some researchers attribute three-quarters of the premature deaths in the U.S. Included in this battle are increased risk of hypertension, stroke, diabetes, certain types of cancer, and heart attacks. Over seventy billion dollars a year is spent by the U.S. health care system to deal with obesity and related medical conditions. When scientists looked at the underlying causes of all of the preventable deaths that took place in the United States in 2001 they found that, together, lack of exercise and poor dietary habits were the largest underlying cause of death. Smoking was the second largest.

The MacArthur Foundation Study showed that there is a simple, basic fact about exercise and your health: "Fitness cuts your risk of dying. It doesn't get much more bottom line than that."

If fear moves you like it does me, put down that cookie and read on while you walk around and burn a few calories.

Help is on the way. A growing body of knowledge shouts in a loud convincing voice, "You can turn it around!" You can bury your toxic waist before it buries you. We don't have to work that hard to improve our health and lose weight.

Not only is it safe to exercise, there is danger in not exercising. "The good news is that people can benefit from even moderate levels of physical activity," says the Surgeon General of the United States.

Physical activity is a term being used more and more by public health professionals, and has proven to be connected with living longer and weight loss. Activities include gardening, playing with your children or grandchildren, and dancing. Almost any physical movement shows definite benefits. These professionals are telling us a little activity is better than none. More activity is even better to regulate your weight, but if you can't or won't be more active, please do something.

Doctors Peter and Lorna Francis are world-renowned fitness scientists. In their book IF IT HURTS DON'T DO IT, they say if your goal is to be healthier and lose some weight (fat), you've been working too hard. I repeat – TOO HARD. They say for permanent weight loss, moderation in your exercise or activity program works best. During low to moderate exercise the body burns a greater proportion of fat than it does during higher intensity workouts. The frequency and duration of your physical activity are more important than high intensity.

For many of us "Life Big Ends at 40" or even sooner. So how do we get back on the straight and narrow? Knowing now that many of us have been working out too hard, how do we start on this new path to weight loss and better health?

First we change our school of thought. We change from the George Bernard Shaw School that says, "Every time I feel like exercising, I lie down until the feeling goes away," and we enroll in the school of Applied Parts. Goethe said it this way:

"Whatever you can do
Or think you can,
Begin it:
Boldness has genius,
Power and Magic in it."

Get off your fanny and onto a lifetime habit of eating well, plus a physical activity program. The human body was meant to move.

To motivate yourself to start is very simple. You use whatever works for you. If fear moves you, go with it. Maybe guilt will work. How about hate? If you hate your appearance, let that motivate you. A desire to feel better is the answer for some.

The most successful motivator of all is pleasure. If you pick movement activities you like, two or three or more for variety, you have the best chance of sticking with a fitness program.

Your level of fitness is your personal declaration of independence. The level you set as your goal is entirely up to you.

Once you have pushed your motivation button, get a go-ahead from your doctor or family physician. Have him/her check out all your systems, especially if you've been a couch veggie for any length of time.

Here we go. Grab any friend – look 'em in the eye and say "TO HEALTH WITH YOU!" If you have a friend or two along, you'll have more fun, and studies show you'll have a better chance of sticking with your program.

Start each day's activity period with stretching. Stretching prepares the muscles for movement. It helps prevent injuries and, done correctly, feels terrific. Stretching has nothing to do with whether or not you can touch your toes. It's not about how far – it's about how it feels.

> **"Get off your fanny and onto a lifetime habit of eating well plus a physical activity program. The human body was meant to move."**

And if it hurts, don't do it. Pain is the body's defense warning system. It tells you to stop, you've stretched too far. The best way to learn a relaxing, pain-free stretching method is to get a copy of Bob Anderson's book or tape called "Stretching". He has sold over a million copies. You'll learn that stretching is not a concentrated effort; it is an effortless concentration. Stretch each day before and after your physical activity. You can stretch any time of day or night to help you relax and deal with the stress in your life. Accompany it with your favorite relaxing music and you'll be delighted with the comfort zone it puts you in.

After stretching to prepare for exercise, comes aerobics or as the doctors Francis prescribe, pre-aerobics. Socialize with family or friends during this activity, whether walking, stationary biking, swimming, etc. Put the emphasis on being kind to yourself. Five to ten minutes every other day to start with. Have a goal of thirty minutes a day, five to six times a week. Keep listening to your body. It's the best speedometer you have. It will be sending signals to your brain all the tim – signals telling you how well your body's systems are working. It will tell you if any adjustments in the duration or intensity of your activity should be made.

There is an easy way to tell if you are exercising fast enough or too hard. If you cannot carry on a conversation during your activity, you are going too fast. If you can sing you are not working hard enough. And if it hurts – DON'T DO IT!

Vary your activity every other week or every other session. Walk, then two days later swim, then you can exercise while you are cleaning the house or working in the garden. Variety is the spice of exercise. Happiness is not the goal – happiness is the way.

When you feel like a new challenge, like making your activity a little more strenuous, make it a gradual, careful progression. Hurry causes hurt. After a week or two, add two or three minutes to your exercise period. You can add a small hill on your walk or carry a small weight on your walk. Increase your burning of calories without straining or hurting yourself.

If you choose a weight-bearing activity (walking, rope skipping, cleaning house, climbing stairs) comfortable, good supporting, well-fitting shoes are important. Shoes come in all colors and are specialized for most activities.

Don't exercise in a wet suit or any clothing that doesn't breathe... cotton tee shirts and cotton sweatshirts are absorbent and allow the body to cool off and not overheat.

Avoid exercising during the heat of the day and pay attention to the weather. Do your activity inside if it is raining or snowing, too hot, or too cold. This is about being kind to yourself.

Stretching, pre-aerobics and next comes strength exercises and weight training, at least twice a week. These exercises strengthen and tone your lean body muscle mass. Muscle burns calories, so your muscles help to maintain a healthy weight. The more muscle you have the bigger your engine to burn calories. Adding lean muscle is like replacing a four-cylinder engine with a six or a V-8 engine. You'll burn more fuel (calories). Ten to fifteen minutes, two or three times a week, is a good start for weight training.

Use light weights and do the exercises slowly. You control the weight. If you can't do the exercise six times, the weight is too heavy. Do not try this without getting instruction or reading up on the subject. Governor Arnold Schwarzenegger has good books for beginners – one for men and one for women. Most gyms and health clubs provide instruction. A personal trainer can be a big help. For muscle strength, weight loss and maintenance, and to prevent osteoporosis, a progressive resistance weight-training program is a must.

Some women are concerned with becoming muscle-bound, gaining too much from weight training. Not to worry. It won't happen unless you take testosterone shots and devote four to eight hours a day to pumping iron. Leave that to the body builders. This is about weight loss and being kind to ourselves. Exercise to live, not live to exercise.

Next, the fourth and final part of your physical activity is your cool-down. Do five minutes of slow stretching with your favorite relaxing music. Then jump in the shower or tub and pat yourself on the back for caring enough to start on the path toward a healthier you.

"You do this for yourself," says John Foreyt, Ph.D., Director of Behavioral Modification

Research Center at Baylor College of Medicine, in Houston, Texas. "You don't exercise for your doctor, not for your spouse, and not to look better for others. You exercise to increase your quality of life and give yourself control over your lifestyle."

That control over your lifestyle includes controlling what you eat or don't eat and when you eat it.

"Eat, Drink, and Be Healthy," written by Walter C. Willett, M.D., is by far the best source of scientifically backed information on nutrition. Dr. Willett and his colleagues at Harvard Medical School and the Harvard School of Public Health have backed all their nutritional facts with large (deep and wide) studies. They have thrown out the misinformed USDA Food Pyramid and replaced it with their new "Healthy Eating Pyramid". The authors have no axe to grind for special interest groups with messages like "Got Milk?" and "What's For Dinner – Beef?"

Dr. Willett and his colleagues have built their "Healthy Eating Pyramid" on a totally new foundation, namely, "daily exercise and weight control." Do read this book!

Diets don't work for weight loss and for keeping weight off. We need to change our lifelong habits of eating more calories than we burn. The body will store the excess calories as body fat.

So many Americans are fat because they eat too much, and too much of the wrong things, and don't do any physical activity. In the American diet, eating refined carbohydrates like flour and sugars is the main cause of obesity. We can lose weight by reducing the amount we eat of these foods, and replacing them with whole grain products and fruit.

Cutting down on portion sizes works for weight loss. Cut down across the nutrition board, which means cutting down on portions from all food groups so we maintain a healthy balance.

Eat a variety of foods that give you pleasure from eating. Eat less red meat and more fish and poultry. Eat a higher percent of fresh foods and a lower percent of processed foods. Cut out snacking and cut down on soft drinks (too much refined sugars and salt). Drink six to eight glasses of pure water a day. Drink bottled water or put a purifying system on your tap.

Get a copy of Dr. Willett's book. It will not only answer all your nutrition questions, it will also give you a variety of healthy, appetizing recipes. Your new eating habits will cut down your calories and it won't take away the pleasure of eating.

Another book to read is Dr. Phil McGraw's "The Ultimate Weight Solution – The Seven Keys to Weight Loss Freedom." His book has been given the usual blast-off in sales after his appearances on "Oprah" and "The Today Show." His weight loss solution has a proven success rate.

The first week you start exercising and eating well, you will lose weight pretty fast. Some of that weight will be water loss. After the first week, a loss of a half-pound to a pound a week is the best rate to lose weight and keep it off.

Your mirror and the fit of your clothes are better ways to tell if you are taking off fat than your bathroom scales. You can lose fat and gain muscle weight. It is possible to become smaller around and weigh about the same. Muscle weighs more than fat. It takes up less space.

Get on with it! Dr. Wayne Dyer says, "Don't let an old person move into your body!" It is never too late or too soon to start. My grandmother, at the age of eighty started walking a mile a day and today, ten years later, we have no idea where she is. Like the commercial says, "Just Do IT!"

Set some short term goals – reasonable goals like: "I am going to lose five pounds in five weeks," or "I am going to walk around the block three times a day for two weeks," or "I am going to eat only one dessert a week for a month." Keep track of your goals and then set new goals. Keep at it and you will feel more energetic and raise the quality of your life. You will have rewritten your personal Declaration of Independence.

Orson Wells' doctor warned him to give up those dinners for four, unless three other people were eating with him. He didn't listen. Did you ever notice how much of the word FATAL is FAT? Sixty percent!

Remember, the human body has a very short shelf life. What is the expiration date on your container?

William Shakespeare said it all when asked what he thought about being fit. He said:

"Being fit?"
"To be or not?
To be!
That is the answer!"

CHAPTER 62
HAVE BEARD WILL TRAVEL

Studs Terkel wrote a book called, "Working". It is the most depressing book I've ever read. Studs went out on the city streets and country roads of the United States, and randomly interviewed people.

He'd go up to people- strangers - and ask them two questions. He'd ask, "What do you do for a living; what work do you do?" and "How do you feel about the work you do."

He asked adults of all races, religions, men and women, tall and short, skinny and fat, rich and poor, young and old, friendly and unfriendly. After asking hundreds of people these two questions, he put their answers in his book. He used the answers from about one hundred fifty people. The results...

Most of us in this country spend most of our lives working at jobs we don't like. That's not strong enough. We do jobs we dislike. We hate our work.

That's sad, very sad. There were a few folks that had jobs they enjoyed. I can remember only three out of the one hundred fifty.

One was a fireman. His answer, "I saved a three-year-old boy from dying last week. I feel pretty good about that!" "I exercise daily to be ready when people need help and I have the respect of the men and women I work with."

The second was a hooker, a prostitute. When asked, "Why do you do it?" She answered, "Just lucky I guess?"

The third person in the book that enjoyed what he did for a living was an actor, Rip Torn. Yes, that's his real name, Riply Torn. He's had a wonderful forty-five year career. He not only likes his work, he loves it. He's saddest when he's not working.

I feel the same about acting. Someone said, "To live a happy life, the secret is to blur the line between work and play." An actor's work is called play. That's a good start in the blurring process.

In forty-five years I've had the privilege of working with many different people. Almost all of them not only wanted to be at

> ## "Most of us in this country spend most of our lives working at jobs we don't like."

that job, they enjoyed the work. Being around content workers is contagious.

If you like variety in your work you might look into acting. For almost half a century when I have said, "Honey, I'm off to the office." I could mean: Palm Springs, Paris, London, Tampa, Las Vegas, Studio City, San Pedro Harbor, Joshua Tree National Forrest, Hawaii, the San Bernardino Mountains, Lone Pine, Disney Studios, The Queen Mary, Warner Ranch, Malibu Beach, Venice Beach, Paramount Studios, CBS/NBC/ABC Studios, Santa Fe, Monument Valley, Lake Powell, Mendocino, Durango, Acapulco, Flagstaff, Taos, Sedona, Ship Rock, Gallup, Valley of Fires, Red Rock Canyon, White Sands, Vasquez Rocks Park, Victoria Island, Calgary, Vancouver, The Straights of Juan de Fucha, New York City, L.A., Kanab, Madison, Alaska, Seattle, San Francisco, Acoma - the oldest town in the U.S., MGM, Columbia Studios, Universal Studios, Warner Brothers Studio, Goldwyn Studios and LAX. There were more but you can imagine the view from my desk.

If Studs had interviewed me, I'd be the fourth person in his book that loved his work.

CHAPTER 63
GOOD LUCK

There are lots of talented people in Hollywood - in front of the camera and behind it. There are a few no-talent folks too. I guess that's true in many businesses. George Carlin says, "You don't have to know what you're doing to do what you're doing today."

My ex-wife was on Broadway. She starred in "No Strings" and at sixty plus, she stars in "The Palm Springs Follies." Sings and dances – she's one of the talented ones.

According to her, my career has been mostly luck. I can't understand why.

The United Airlines – Pratt and Whitney TV commercial I did was because I could carry an actress on my left shoulder and an actor on my right shoulder and walk up the steps to a 747. Talk about talent.

In the L'OR Coffee commercial I did in London and Paris, I was cast because I looked like the fella who started the company. He had been dead for about two hundred years. Not just every actor has that talent.

After I auditioned for the "Fruit of The Loom" underwear TV spot they asked me to stand and stretch my arms out to the side. Then they measured my wingspan from fingertip to fingertip. They had made a chest of drawers and were looking for an actor who could reach both ends of it and pick it up and move it while looking for his shorts. Got that job solely on talent. I had the talent of wearing thirty-eight-inch sleeves.

> "They had made a chest of drawers and were looking for an actor who could reach both ends of it and pick it up and move it while looking for his shorts. Got that job solely on talent."

That day, forty-five years ago on Sunset Boulevard, in Hollywood, while moving furniture, when the talent agent handed me his card and said to call him – what a stroke of talent that was.

When I took a screen test to be under contract to MGM with extensive training as a basketball player – luck? – I think not. George Cukor directed the test. Now I ask you, how unlucky can you get? But talent will win out.

I was a contract player at Universal Studios when "Wagon Train" was in its glory. I got a small part to play in one episode. I was so bad in the part, the studio was going to let me go. Ward Bond said, "Give the kid another chance!" One hundred and ten episodes later I had worked with most of the big stars in Hollywood. Luck? Don't be silly.

Fourteen years ago, my agent sent me on an audition for the role of "The Gorton's Fisherman." I had a beard at the time and he asked me to shave it off. I was the only bearded actor at the interview. They must have read hundreds of guys. This is my fourteenth year as their spokesman. Gorton's changed their logo to a bearded fisherman. That's not luck. That's chin hair-growing talent!

Still, my ex insists, that as far as my career goes, I have a horseshoe up a certain orifice of my body.

I didn't have the luck to have a parent or an uncle who was a movie star or some successful director or producer or a head of some studio like MGM or Columbia in the family. Nope, never relied on nepotism.

I never got in with the Hollywood social scene and wasn't wealthy enough to buy a part or pay for a flashy PR campaign. Stayed away from the casting couch. Never got represented by one of the big powerful agencies, the ones that can arrange "package deals." With one Sinatra you have to take two trained dogs and one Denny Miller.

Wasn't a member of "The John Wayne Players"... sure would liked to have been. Wait a minute... How'd I do two hundred and thirty-six TV episodes, nineteen feature films and over two hundred TV commercial spots? You don't think luck had something to do with it? You don't think my ex could be right?

To quote my favorite actress, Katharine Hepburn, "No one does it alone. Your success belongs to the people who are holding you up. I can only say that I am the product of adorable people. I've been so lucky, just lucky."

He looks familiar...
It's... um...
what's his name...
you know...
the Fish stick guy.

CHAPTER 64
DIDN'T YOU USED TO BE

You were on "Wagon Train" and "Dallas" and the two islands — Gillgan's and Fantasy. Weren't you on "Magnum PI," "Gunsmoke?" And weren't you Tarzan and the Brawny Paper Towel Giant and the The Gorton's Fisherman? And, didn't you work with Peter Sellers, Tom Selleck, Charles Bronson, Dennis Weaver, Bette Davis, Rhonda Fleming, Robert Ryan, Barbara Stanwick, James Garner, Ward Bond, Larry Hagman, Juliet Prowse, Bob Hope, Lucille Ball, Frank Sinatra and Dean Martin and Shirley MacLaine, Bill Bixby, Dennis Hopper and Stacy Keach and Margo Kidder and Jason Robards, John McIntyre, and...

What IS your name?

That's what character actors do – they disappear right before your very eyes!

40

41

DENNY MILLER
FILM AND TELEVISION CREDITS

STAR OR GUEST STAR BILLING:

Life of Riley
Northwest Passage
Overland Trail
Laramie (2)
Riverboat
Have Gun, Will Travel
G.E. Theater
The Deputy
Wells Fargo
Richard Diamond
Rifleman
Wagon Train (107)
Girl From U.N.C.L.E.
Ben Casey
Gilligan's Island (2)
Death Valley Days (2)
High Chaparral
Hawaii Five-0
Mona McClusky
Fugitive
The Name of the Game
Love American Style
I Dream of Jeannie
Canon
My Friend Tony

I Spy
Keeper of the Wild
Dr. Quinn (2 parter)
Ironsides
Mobile ONE
Gunsmoke
McLeod
Brady Bunch
Dusty's Trail
Sheriff Lobo
Emergency
Wonder Woman
Class of '62
Quincy
Fall Guy (2)
Voyager
Family Films
Flying High
Hart to Hart
Barnaby Jones (2)
The Runaways
Knight Rider
Alice
Bronk
Big Island

The Outlaws
Vegas (2)
Stone
Young Maverick
Border Town (2)
Fantasy Island
Ten Speed & Brown Shoe
Beyond Westworld
Flo
When the Whistle Blows
Mash
6 Million Dollar Man
Buck Rogers
House Calls
Magnum PI (3)
Today's FBI
Battlestar Galactica (2)
Rockford Files (2)
Simon & Simon
Matt Houston (2)
The Incredible Hulk (2)
Dallas (4)
Hardcastle and
    McCormick
Streets of San Francisco (2)

STAR OR GUEST STAR BILLING:

continued...

Doctor in the House
Black's Magic
Murder She Wrote

Charlie's Angels (3)
Werewolf
Sea Hunt

Wagon Train Special
Lonesome Dove (3)

FEATURES:

Tarzan the Ape-man
Some Came Running
Love in a Gold Fish Bowl
The Party
Making It
Buck and the Preacher
Island at the Top of the
    World

Nick and Nora
The Norseman
The Dion Brothers
Dr. Death
Armageddon
Vanished
Cabo Blanco
Mystique

The Seal
Shooting Stars
"V"
Mickey Spillane

DENNY MILLER
COMMERCIAL CREDITS

Kools

TWA

Continental Airlines

Brawney Paper Towels (12)

Slamback (with Lucille Ball)

Hamm's Beer

Miller's High Life (8)

Pepsi

Waring Blender

Arby's Restaurants (3)

Clorox

Champion Spark Plugs

Bank of America

Strohs Beer

Salem Cigarettes

Fruit of the Loom

Prestone II (10)

Big Wally (13)

Gorton's Spokesman (14 years)

Jack in the Box

United – Pratt & Whitney

Harvey's Bristol Creme

Kismet Games

Plymouth Fury

Phoenix Bank

Skippers (3; plus 3 radio)

Frozen Enchiladas (2)

Pizza

Delco Shock Absorbers

Texaco (with Bob Hope)

Risk

L'or French Coffee (4)

West German Cigarettes (25)

Nissan Pathfinder (2)

Backwoods Cigar (2)

U.S. Marine Corps (4)

U.S. Air Force (10)

AFTER WORD

*"Acting is the most minor of gifts
and not a very high-class way to make a living.
After all, Shirley Temple could do it at age four."*

–Katharine Hepburn